making handmade

Lampwork Beads
& Glass Jewelry

Creative Publishing international

First published in the United States of America by
Creative Publishing international, Inc., a member of
Quayside Publishing Group
400 First Avenue North
Suite 300
Minneapolis, MN 55401
1-800-328-3895
www.creativepub.com

ISBN-13: 978-1-58923-391-1
ISBN-10: 1-58923-391-3

10 9 8 7 6 5 4 3 2 1

Library of Congress Cataloging-in-Publication Data
Ronat, Hava.
  Making handmade lampwork beads and glass jewelry / Hava Ronat and Danny Ronat.
     p. cm.
  Includes bibliographical references and index.
  ISBN 978-1-58923-391-1 (alk. paper)
  1. Beadwork. 2. Beads. 3. Jewelry making. I. Ronat, Danny. II. Title.

  TT860.R83 2008
   739.27--dc22   2008015275
                                                        CIP

Editor: Shoshana Brickman
Book Design: Eddie Goldfine
Page Layout: Ariane Rybski
Photographs: Liah Chesnokov and Hagit Goren

Printed in Singapore

making handmade

Lampwork Beads
& Glass Jewelry

Hava & Danny Ronat

Creative Publishing
international

Contents

Introduction

In this book, you'll be guided on how to make fabulous handmade glass beads, and use them to string colorful, unique pieces of jewelry. In **Part 1: Making Glass Beads**, you'll find step-by-step instructions for making more than twenty dazzling glass bead designs. Of course, you can make countless variations by changing the color, size, or shape of any of these beads. In **Part 2: Glass Bead Jewelry**, you'll find instructions for necklaces, bracelets, earrings, and brooches using the beads described in Part 1, as well as diverse store-bought beads. Even if you haven't mastered the techniques described in Part 1, you can still complete the projects in Part 2—simply substitute the handmade glass beads with similar store-bought varieties.

About the Authors

Hava and Danny Ronat are a husband-and-wife team who combine distinct skills and experience to create a beautiful array of glass beads. Hava is a beadmaker, painter, and graphic designer who studied art at the Avni Institute in Tel Aviv and the Art Institute of Chicago. Danny is a mechanical engineer who became enchanted by glass after working in stained glass as a hobby. Together, they operate a successful handmade jewelry shop in Neve Tzedek, Tel Aviv, Israel.

Materials and Tools

Many of the items described below relate specifically to glass bead making, and they can be found in specialty glass shops and online. Items used for making the jewelry projects can be found in bead shops, crafts stores, and online.

Bead annealer This large kilnlike container can be used to gradually cool warm glass beads. It is suitable for cooling beads of all sizes.

Bead rake This hooked metal tool is used to poke holes and drag lines in warm glass (see Figures G–I on page 9).

Bead reamer This tool can be used to clean the inside of handmade glass beads after they have been removed from the mandrel, and to smooth rough edges of glass.

Bead separator This powder is used to coat the top 3" (76 mm) of mandrels so that beads can be removed after they have been cooled.

Beading wire A variety of wires and threads are used to string beads. Be sure to select durable, high-quality materials.

Beading wire

Caliper This can be used to measure and help you make identically sized beads (see Figure P on page 9).

Electric grinder This can be used to clean the inside of handmade beads after they have been removed from the mandrel, and to smooth rough edges of glass.

Enamel powder This is made from finely ground colored glass. A thin layer of enamel powder on a bead surface can intensify color, add new color, or create a dusted effect.

Fiber blankets Made from insulating ceramic fibers, these blankets are used to gradually cool warm glass beads (see photo page 15).

Flat file This is used to file the top and bottom of handmade glass beads and to smooth rough edges (see Figure B on page 9).

Flattener This tweezer-like tool has two flat sides that are pressed together to squeeze and flatten hot beads (see Figure L on page 9).

Glass This remarkable, colorful, and versatile material, made from a mixture of sand, potash and lime, is melted to make the beads in this book. Different formulas may be used to make glass, which affects the temperature at which the glass expands and contracts as it is heated and cooled. Glass is categorized by its coefficient of expansion (COE). For the projects in this book, use relatively soft glass (with a COE of about 104). Harder glass (with a lower COE) requires greater heat to melt. When using several colors of glass in a

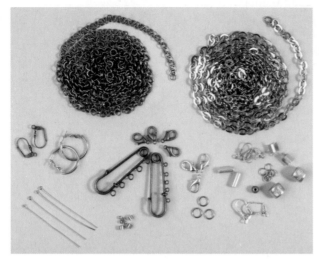
Jewelry findings

Glass rods

Flat glass

single bead, *make sure every color has the same COE.* Most of the projects in this book use **glass rods**. These are available in an endless array of colors. Most glass rods have a diameter of about ¼" (6 mm) and they come in various lengths. Thinner rods of glass are called stringers (see page 20 for how to make a stringer). All glass changes color when it is heated. Most glass returns to the same color after it cools. Glass that is called "striking" glass changes color permanently after it has been heated. Strips of **flat glass** (measuring about ¼" to ⅜" [6 to 10 mm]) can also be used to make beads.

Glass rod cutter A tool used to cut rods of glass (see Figure O on page 9).

Graphite paddle or block This is used to shape and manipulate warm beads. They can be found in various shapes and sizes (see Figures C and F on page 9).

Jewelry findings A wide array of silver and gold chains, pins, clasps, and crimps beads are used to assemble the jewelry projects. Be sure to select durable, high-quality materials.

Knives and blades These are used to carve and pull warm bead while making glass beads (see Figure Q on page 9).

Leaf masher This tweezer-like tool has two textured sides that are pressed together to make a leaflike impression on hot glass (see Figure N on page 9).

Mandrel This stainless steel rod is the base upon which glass is wound to form a bead. Mandrels come in lengths ranging from 9" to 12" (23 to 31 cm) and diameters ranging from ¹⁄₁₆" to ³⁄₁₆" (2 to 5 mm). The diameter of the mandrel determines the size of the bead hole. All projects in this book are wound on a ³⁄₃₂" (3 mm) mandrel, unless otherwise stated.

Mandrel block This wooden block has several holes for supporting mandrels that have been dipped in a bead separator until they are ready to be used. To make your own mandrel block, drill several holes on one side of a brick-size block of wood. (Make holes of various sizes to support mandrels of various diameters.)

Marver Made from graphite, steel, or aluminum, this heat-resistant surface is used to roll, press, and shape hot beads. Marvers may be flat or patterned (see Figures D–E).

Metal file This thin twisted file is used to clean the inside of beads (see Figures J–K).

Pliers Various types of pliers are used in these projects. Flat-nose pliers (see Figure T) are used to flatten crimp beads. Round-nose pliers (see Figure U) are used to make loops in head pins and eye pins. Shaping pliers are used to stretch and shape glass (see Figures R–S).

Safety glasses Wear these at all times when making glass beads.

Tool rest This grooved, triangular metal support is used to hold glass rods and other materials when not in use (see Figure A).

Torch A variety of torches are suitable for bead making, and the type you chose depends on your budget and your needs. A **single-fuel torch** (see photo on page 10) is good for beginners. It is relatively

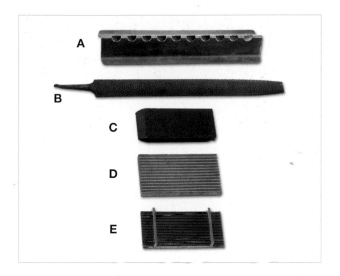

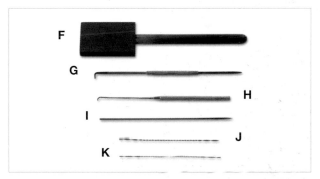

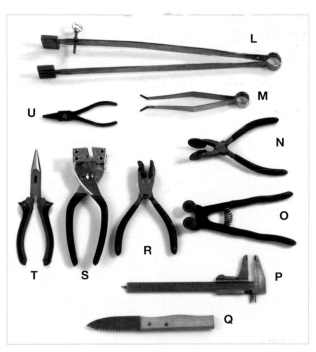

Single-fuel torch

Oxygen-propane torch

inexpensive and can be set up in a very small space. Select one that runs on brazen fuel, a modified propane gas, or a blended fuel, since these reach temperatures that are high enough for working with soft glass. An **oxygen-propane torch** is excellent for beginners and more experienced bead makers since it melts glass more quickly than the single-fuel torch, and its flame can be altered as needed. It requires a large tank and is not very portable. It runs on a combination fuel, can reach very high temperatures, and is appropriate for working with soft or hard glass. *Set up your torch according to the manufacturer's instructions, and have a professional hook up the fuel tanks, if necessary.*

Tweezers These are used to pull molten glass to form stringers and to sprinkle enamel. They can also be used to lift gold leaf when applying it to warm beads (see Figure M on page 9).

Vermiculite This is a natural mineral that expands when heated. A large bowl or pot filled with vermiculite pieces can be used to gradually cool warm beads (see photo page 15).

Wire cutter This is used to cut beading wire and other materials.

Setting up Your Work Area

- Set up your work station in a well-ventilated area. A room with cross ventilation is best, but don't work directly in front of an open window.
- Equip your room with a fire extinguisher, and make sure it is easily accessible from your work station.
- Select a work table that is made from nonflammable material.
- Make sure the height of your work table is appropriate to your height, and sit in a comfortable chair. Take breaks while working to stand up, walk around, and stretch your legs.
- Place materials such as glass rods at a comfortable distance from your dominant hand. Make sure you do not need to pass your hand over the flame to reach these materials while you work.

- Store glass rods in a safe, easily accessible place. Make yourself a customized glass rod shelving unit by gluing together several 10" (25 cm) plastic tubes, and arranging them horizontally on a shelf (see photo page 8). Sort rods according to color.
- Prepare all the materials you will need for your project in advance.

Safety is of utmost importance when working with fire and hot glass.
- Wear safety glasses at all times.
- Tie back long hair, and don't wear scarves or items that dangle.
- Never leave a lit torch unattended.

Work area

Part 1:
Making
Glass Beads

Basic Techniques

The first stage in making glass beads is understanding the total process, which is described below. Once you are familiar with these stages, you'll be ready to wind your first glass bead. Make a few basic round beads by following the step-by-step guidelines on pages 16 and 17. Once you are comfortable with this process, practice making the shaped beads described on pages 18 and 19. Learn how to make a stringer, the thin glass rod used to decorate beads, on page 20. From here, the sky is the limit, and with a little practice and patience, you'll be able to make all of the beads described throughout this chapter. Please note that the glass bead projects are arranged in order from easier to more challenging.

Preparing the mandrels

Make sure all mandrels are clean and straight, as it is difficult (and sometimes impossible) to remove cooled beads from bent mandrels. Dip top 3" (76 mm) of each mandrel into bead separator, then insert mandrels, dipped-side up, into mandrel block. Leave mandrels to air dry (or fire dry them using a torch) before starting. Do not attempt to work on a mandrel until bead separator is completely dry. *Always have several prepared mandrels on hand before you start winding beads.*

Lighting the torch

Use a striker or lighter to light torch. To light a **single-fuel torch**, open valve by turning it one-quarter turn counterclockwise. Bring striker about 1" (2.5 cm) from top of torch and depress striker. Once torch flame ignites, adjust valve until flame is light blue. To turn off torch, turn valve clockwise all the way.

To light an **oxygen–propane torch**, turn gas valve first by turning it counterclockwise for a one-quarter turn. Bring striker about 1" (2.5 cm) from top of torch and depress striker. Once torch flame ignites and there is an orange flame, open oxygen valve, and adjust both valves until there is a stable light blue flame. To turn off torch, close oxygen valve first, then propane valve. Make sure valves are securely closed after turning off torch. If you hear the hiss of oxygen or smell gas, there may be a fuel leak, so have torch checked by a professional immediately. *If you have any mishaps or doubts about the safety of your torch, have it checked immediately by a professional.* Never leave a lit torch unattended, and remember that a torch remains hot for about 15 minutes after use.

Winding the bead

Both mandrel and glass rod must be heated before winding a bead. Be sure to keep bead warm throughout winding process, since cooling it suddenly can cause thermal shock. Thermal shock may cause bead to crack immediately or several days after it is finished. Rotate bead constantly while winding so that it doesn't sag (because of gravity) or become overheated on one side.

Decorating and shaping the bead

Always keep base bead warm (hold it at edge of flame) while heating rods or stringers for adding decorations. After bead has been decorated, flame-cut rod (or stringer) by turning rod toward you as you rotate bead away from you. Allow flame to cut through rod completely before removing rod from heat. Always make sure a bead is slightly firm before shaping it against a graphite paddle, marver, or flattener. Since contact with any of these tools causes that area of the bead to cool, reheat bead gently immediately after shaping it (by passing it in and out of flame a few times) to prevent thermal shock. Don't overheat bead, since you don't want to melt away the shape.

Cooling the bead

When bead is finished, hold it at edge of flame until glow fades and bead firms. Transfer to cooling material to slow down cooling process and prevent thermal shock. Make sure warm bead is firm before transferring it to this material; otherwise, fibers from the blanket may stick to the warm glass. Do not allow warm beads to touch each other as they dry. Small and medium-size beads (all of the beads in this book) may be cooled properly using fiber blankets or a vermiculite-filled container. Larger beads should be cooled in a bead annealer.

Removing the bead from the mandrel

Most beads can be removed simply by twisting them with your fingers as you hold mandrel with pliers. If bead doesn't budge, try holding mandrel with a vice-grip as you twist. If this doesn't work, place bead in water for a minute or two to soften bead separator; then twist off bead. When removing bead from mandrel, take care not to bend mandrel.

Cleaning and filing the bead

To remove bead separator residue left in bead hole, draw bead reamer in and out of the bead hole a few times; then rinse bead with water. Repeat until bead is clean. If there are sharp edges on top or bottom of bead, file them down with an electrical grinder or flat file. Take care not to file bead too much, since this can dull its glossy finish.

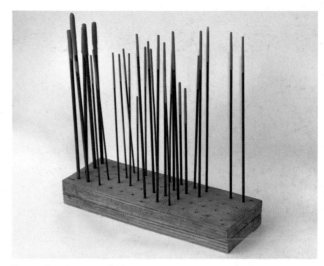
Preparing the mandrels

Cooling beads with vermiculite

Cooling beads using fiber blankets

Round Bead

Materials and Tools

- pale amber glass rod
- mandrel dipped in bead separator
- torch
- 2 fiber blankets

1. Hold glass rod in dominant hand and mandrel in other hand. Put tip of rod into flame and heat gently until glowing. Rotate rod as it heats, so that it heats evenly.

TIP Don't heat glass too quickly, as this can cause thermal shock.

2. Heat rod while turning until molten and glowing. Bring mandrel into cooler part of flame (behind glass rod), and heat gently.

TIP Both mandrel and glass must be heated, as molten glass won't stick to a cold mandrel.

3. Touch the tip to the mandrel. If the glass doesn't stick, heat glass and mandrel a little more.

4. If glass sticks, begin winding bead by slowly turning mandrel away from you. This draws molten glass over top of mandrel, so that bead is wound toward you. Hold mandrel steady as you rotate it, so that glass makes a tidy ring around mandrel.

5. When ring is complete, separate rod from glass on mandrel by holding rod in flame as you wind mandrel away from you. The heated area of the rod will get increasingly thin until rod and bead are completely separated.

6. Rotate mandrel in flame to heat glass evenly and gently until surface is smooth and rounded.

TIP Don't pull rod away until it has been flame-cut, as this may leave a thin string of glass.

7. To build up bead, bring rod back into flame and heat tip until molten. Continue heating base bead by holding it at edge of flame. Take care not to overheat bead, as you don't want base bead to sag or lose its shape.

8. Touch molten tip to base bead and wind another ring of glass on top of first ring. Flame-cut when ring is complete.

TIP Keep mandrel in constant motion while building up bead, otherwise gravity will draw warm glass downward.

9. Repeat steps 7 and 8 until bead is desired size.

10. Move bead to edge of flame until glow fades and bead firms up.

TIP Don't allow glass to cool too quickly, as this can cause thermal shock.

11. When glow fades, transfer bead to fiber blankets and set aside to cool completely.

Bold Beaded Ball Necklace *(see page 95)*

Cylindrical Bead

Materials and Tools

- medium red glass rod
- mandrel dipped in bead separator
- torch

- graphite paddle
- 2 fiber blankets

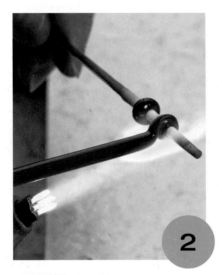

2

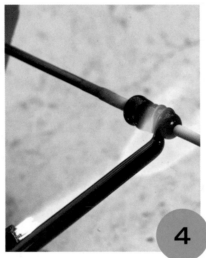

4

6

1. Wind an 8mm round bead (see steps 1 to 8, pages 16–17) with medium red glass.

2. Leave a space of ⁵⁄₁₆" (8 mm) on mandrel, then wind a second, similar bead.

3. Fill in space between beads by winding more glass.

4. Heat bead evenly until glass fuses to form a single cylindrical bead.

5. Cool bead slightly, then roll gently on graphite paddle to shape a smooth cylinder. Roll top and bottom of bead against edge of graphite paddle to even up ends.

6. Heat bead gently until surface is smooth.

7. Move bead to edge of flame to cool until glow fades. Sandwich bead between fiber blankets and set aside to cool completely.

Bicone Bead

Materials and Tools

- dark ivory glass rod
- mandrel dipped in bead separator
- torch
- graphite paddle
- 2 fiber blankets

1.

3.

5.

1. Wind a round bead (see steps 1 to 8, pages 16–17) that is a little longer than desired bead, and a little thicker around middle.

2. Cool bead slightly, then bring one end of bead into flame and heat until glowing.

3. Roll glowing end at an angle on graphite paddle to form a cone shape.

4. Heat this end of bead gently until surface is smooth.

5. Heat other end of bead until glowing, then roll this end at an angle on graphite paddle to form a cone shape.

6. Heat this end of bead gently until surface is smooth.

7. Repeat steps 2 to 6 until bead is symmetrical. Gently heat entire bead until surface is smooth.

8. Move bead to edge of flame to cool until glow fades. Sandwich between fiber blankets and set aside to cool completely.

Stringer

Materials and Tools

- petroleum green glass rod
- torch
- tweezers or bent-nose pliers

1. Heat tip of glass rod until a small ball of molten glass forms.

2. Use tweezers to pinch a small amount of molten glass.

3. Allow glow to fade a little (this just takes a second) then pull glass into a thin straight strand.

TIP Glass cools quickly as it is pulled, making it increasingly difficult to pull. The quicker you pull the glass, the thinner the stringer.

4. Hold pulled glass straight as it cools. (Straight stringers are easier to use than bent ones.)

5. Flame-cut stringer from rod and set aside to cool.

TIP Since stringers are much thinner than rods, they heat faster. When decorating with stringers, heat at edge of flame, so that they do not become too soft.

Porcupine Bead

Materials and Tools

- pale amber glass rod
- mandrel dipped in bead separator
- torch
- 2 fiber blankets

1. Wind a 12mm round bead (see steps 1 to 8, pages 16–17) with amber glass.

2. Cool bead at edge of flame until firm.

3. Keep bead warm, and heat tip of amber rod until molten.

4. Touch molten tip to bead so that rod is perpendicular to bead.

5. Draw rod away from bead while rotating bead forward. Flame-cut rod, leaving a single dot on bead.

6. Turn mandrel so that dot is at top of bead, and allow dot to sink a little into bead surface.

7. Repeat steps 2 to 5 to make several dots on bead surface.

8. Heat bead gently until dots are rounded but not absorbed.

9. Move bead to edge of flame to cool until glow fades. Sandwich bead between fiber blankets and set aside to cool completely.

Dot Size

The size of the dot depends on how much molten glass is left on the bead. This depends on how the long molten tip is pressed onto the base bead, and how much pressure is applied.

Symmetrical Dots

Dots do not need to be symmetrical, but symmetry can add to the beauty of a design. To make evenly spaced symmetrical dots, put a dot on bead, then put a dot on mandrel that is in line with dot on bead. (Be sure to place dot on mandrel on an area covered with bead separator.) Turn bead 180 degrees and place dot directly opposite first dot. You won't be able to see dot on bead anymore, but you will be able to see dot on mandrel, and this will help you line up the second dot. Now you have two reference points on your bead. Fill in spaces between these dots with evenly spaced dots.

Flush Dotted Bead

This technique is identical to the one used to make the **Porcupine Bead** (see above), only the bead is heated until dots are absorbed and bead surface is smooth.

Dotted Sandwich Bead

Materials and Tools

- medium grass green glass rod
- white glass rod
- gold pink striking glass rod
- light emerald green glass rod
- mandrel dipped in bead separator
- torch
- marver
- 2 fiber blankets

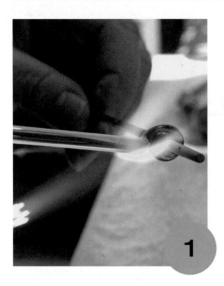

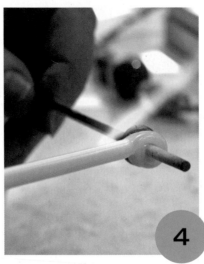

1. Wind a 12mm round bead (see steps 1 to 8, pages 16–17) with medium grass green glass.

2. Cool bead at edge of flame until firm.

3. Keep bead warm, and heat tip of white rod until molten.

4. Wind a white bead immediately beside green bead. The white bead should be slightly longer than green bead but have the same diameter.

5. Heat beads gently until they fuse together.

6. Cool bead slightly; then roll gently on graphite paddle to shape a smooth cylinder. Roll top and bottom of bead against edge of graphite paddle to even up ends.

7. Heat bead gently until surface is smooth, and heat tip of gold pink striking rod until molten.

8. Touch molten tip to white area of bead and wrap around bead until white area is completely covered with pink striking glass.

9. Cool bead slightly, then roll gently on graphite paddle to reshape cylinder. Heat bead gently until surface is smooth.

10. Keep bead warm, and heat tip of light emerald green rod until molten.

11. Touch molten tip to pink area of bead, as close as possible to green area, and make a dot.

12. Repeat step 11 to make a ring of evenly spaced dots on pink side of bead, as close as possible to the green area.

13. Heat bead gently until dots are rounded but not absorbed.

14. Move bead to edge of flame to cool until glow fades Sandwich bead between fiber blankets and set aside to cool completely.

Strawberries in Spring Necklace *(see page 70)*

Dotted Disk Bead

Materials and Tools

- dark aquamarine glass rod
- dark red glass stringer (page 20)
- mandrel dipped in bead separator
- torch
- graphite paddle
- 2 fiber blankets

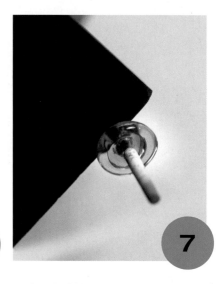

1. Wind an 8mm round bead (see steps 1 to 8, pages 16–17) with dark aquamarine glass.

2. Cool bead at edge of flame until firm.

3. Keep bead warm, and heat tip of dark aquamarine rod until molten.

4. Touch molten tip to bead and wrap a ring of glass around bead. Width of ring should be identical to bead's width, so that bead diameter (not length) increases.

5. Cool bead at edge of flame until firm.

6. Repeat steps 3 and 4 to wrap another ring around bead and form a disk-shaped bead.

7. Cool bead slightly; then roll top and bottom of bead against edge of graphite paddle to flatten.

8. Heat bead gently until surface is smooth, and heat tip of dark red stringer until molten.

TIP Take care not to overheat bead when adding dots, as the disk is quite thin and too much heat will cause it to lose its shape.

9. Touch molten tip to edge of bead and make a dot.

10. Repeat step 9 to make evenly spaced dots around circumference of bead.

11. Heat bead gently until dots are rounded but not absorbed. Heat tip of dark aquamarine rod until molten.

12. Touch molten tip to edge of bead and wind two more rings of glass around bead.

13. Cool bead slightly; then roll top and bottom of bead against graphite paddle to flatten.

14. Repeat steps 8 to 10 to make another ring of dots around circumference of bead.

15. Heat bead gently until dots are rounded but not absorbed.

16. Move bead to edge of flame to cool until glow fades. Sandwich bead between fiber blankets and set aside to cool completely.

Rocky Bead

Materials and Tools

- flat strip of glass, ¼" (6 mm) wide, yellow
- mandrel dipped in bead separator
- torch
- graphite paddle
- 2 fiber blankets

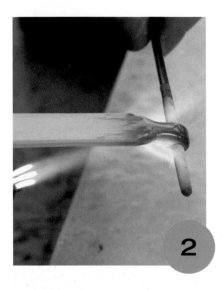

1. Heat tip of glass strip until molten and touch to warm mandrel.

2. Rotate mandrel away from you while holding glass strip steady to form ring of glass around mandrel.

3. Continue heating tip of glass strip as you rotate mandrel until bead is desired size.

4. Cool bead slightly; then press on graphite paddle to shape as desired.

TIP This bead resembles a natural rock, so there is no need to aim for symmetry. Reheat and press bead repeatedly until you achieve the desired shape.

5. Heat bead gently until surface is smooth.

6. Move bead to edge of flame to cool until glow fades. Sandwich between fiber blankets and set aside to cool completely.

Textured Bead

Materials and Tools

- light turquoise glass rod
- transparent glass rod
- mandrel dipped in bead separator
- torch

- graphite paddle
- patterned marver
- 2 fiber blankets

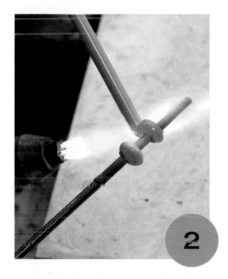

2

4

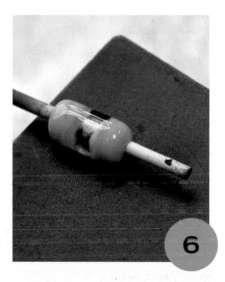

6

1. Wind an 8mm round bead (see steps 1 to 8, pages 16–17) with light turquoise glass.

2. Leave a space of about 5/16" (8 mm) and wind a second, similar bead.

3. Allow beads to cool slightly and heat tip of transparent rod until molten.

4. Wind transparent glass in space between beads to fill space completely.

5. Heat bead evenly until glass fuses to form a single cylindrical bead.

6. Cool bead slightly, then roll gently on graphite paddle to shape a smooth cylinder. Roll top and bottom of bead against edge of graphite paddle to even up ends.

(continued)

7. Hold patterned marver so that it will be at an angle to bead. Heat bead gently then roll on marver in one direction, all the way around, until grooves meet. Do not roll back, since aligning grooves is difficult.

8. Heat bead very gently until surface is smooth. Take care not to overheat as this will cause grooves to disappear.

9. Move bead to edge of flame to cool until glow fades.

10. Sandwich bead between fiber blankets and set aside to cool completely.

Freehand Decorated Bead

Materials and Tools

- dark ivory glass rod
- petroleum green glass stringer (page 20)

- mandrel dipped in bead separator
- torch

- graphite paddle
- 2 fiber blankets

1. Wind a 12mm cylindrical bead (see steps 1 to 6, page 18) with dark ivory glass.

2. Cool bead at edge of flame until firm.

3. Keep bead warm and heat tip of petroleum green stringer until molten.

4. Touch molten tip to bead and draw swirls, stripes, and dots all over bead. Ensure that bead and stringer stay warm at all times.

5. When design is complete, heat bead evenly until design is absorbed and surface is smooth.

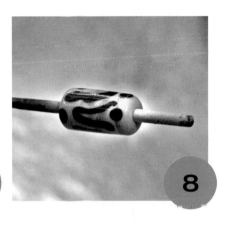

6. Cool bead slightly, then roll gently on graphite paddle to shape a smooth cylinder. Roll top and bottom of bead against edge of graphite paddle to even up ends.

7. Heat bead gently until surface is smooth.

8. Move bead to edge of flame to cool until glow fades. Sandwich bead between fiber blankets and set aside to cool completely.

Eye Bead

Materials and Tools

- ivory glass rod
- light turquoise glass rod
- orange glass rod
- aquamarine glass rod
- mandrel dipped in bead separator
- torch
- bead rake, set in a cup of water
- 2 fiber blankets

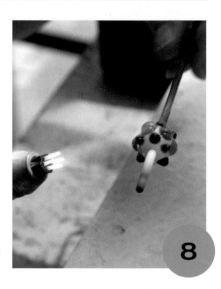

1. Wind a 12mm round bead (see steps 1 to 8, pages 16–17) with ivory glass.

2. Cool bead at edge of flame until firm.

3. Keep bead warm, and heat tip of light turquoise rod until molten.

4. Touch molten tip at middle of bead and make a dot.

5. Repeat step 3 to make a ring of six evenly spaced dots around middle of bead.

6. Heat bead gently until dots are rounded but not absorbed. Heat tip of orange rod until molten.

7. Touch molten tip to bead and make a dot to one side of turquoise dots, and between every two dots.

8. Repeat step 7 to make rings of evenly spaced orange dots on both sides of turquoise dots. Be sure to place each orange dot between two turquoise dots.

9. Heat bead evenly until dots are absorbed and surface is smooth. Cool bead slightly.

10. Heat one turquoise dot until glowing then plunge bead rake into center of dot to make a hole.

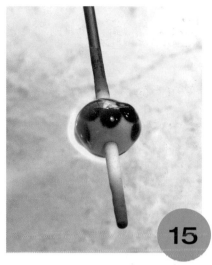

11. Repeat step 10 to make holes in every turquoise dot.

12. Keep bead warm and heat tip of light aquamarine rod to form a small ball of molten glass.

13. Touch molten tip to one hole to form a cap of glass over hole. (You want the glass to cover hole and trap air inside of it rather than fill the hole.)

14. Repeat step 13 to cover each hole with a cap of light aquamarine glass.

15. Heat bead evenly until surface is smooth.

16. Move bead to edge of flame to cool until glow fades. Sandwich bead between fiber blankets and set aside to cool completely.

Turquoise and Coral Harvest Necklace *(see page 113)*

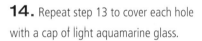

Forget-Me-Not Flower Bead

Materials and Tools

- medium amber glass rod
- jade green in clear filigrana glass rod
- light sky blue glass rod

- dark aquamarine glass rod
- mandrel dipped in bead separator
- torch

- bead rake, set in a cup of water
- 2 fiber blankets

1. Wind a 12mm round bead (see steps 1 to 8, pages 16–17) with medium amber glass.

2. Cool bead at edge of flame until firm.

3. Keep bead warm, and heat tip of jade green in clear filigrana glass rod until molten.

TIP Heat filigrana rod at edge of flame. Take care not to overheat, since this glass is quite sensitive and tends to crack easily.

4. Touch molten tip at one end of bead and draw in diagonal line to other end of bead. Switch directions and draw back in diagonal line to back to other end of bead.

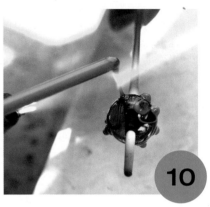

5. Continue in this manner to make a zigzag all around bead. Be sure to end zigzag where it started.

6. Heat bead evenly until zigzag is absorbed and surface is smooth.

7. Cool bead slightly and heat tip of light sky blue rod until molten.

8. Touch molten tip near middle of bead and make a dot.

9. Repeat step 8 to make two more dots, close together but not touching, to form a triangle of dots clustered around middle of bead.

10. Repeat steps 8 and 9 to make three more evenly spaced triangles of dots around middle of bead.

11. Heat bead gently until dots are rounded but not absorbed. Heat tip of dark aquamarine rod until molten. (Heat a smaller part of tip than you did in step 7 because you want these dots to be smaller.)

12. Touch molten tip to one light blue dot to make a smaller dark aquamarine dot.

13. Repeat step 10 to make smaller dark aquamarine dots on each light blue dot.

14. Heat bead evenly until dots are absorbed and surface is smooth. Cool bead slightly.

15. Heat one triangle of dots until glowing, then plunge bead rake into center of triangle to make a hole.

16. Repeat step 15 to make holes in the center of every triangle of dots.

17. Keep bead warm, and heat tip of dark aquamarine rod to form a small ball of molten glass.

18. Touch molten tip to one hole to form a cap of glass over hole. (You want the glass to cover hole and trap air inside of it rather than fill the hole.)

19. Repeat step 16 to cover each hole with a cap of dark aquamarine glass.

20. Heat bead evenly until surface is smooth.

21. Move bead to edge of flame to cool until glow fades. Sandwich bead between fiber blankets and set aside to cool completely.

Forget-Me-Not Bracelet *(see page 101)*

Encased Gold Leaf Bead

Materials and Tools

- gold leaf
- red striking glass rod
- transparent glass rod
- marver
- mandrel dipped in bead separator*

- torch
- graphite paddle
- tweezers
- 2 fiber blankets

* Use a mandrel with a ³⁄₁₆" (5 mm) diameter when winding bead for the Encased Golden Leaf Choker.

1. Position gold leaf on marver so that bead can be rolled from one end of leaf to other in a single motion.

2. Wind a 12mm cylindrical bead (see steps 1 to 5, page 18) with red striking glass.

3. Heat bead until glowing, then lay at one end of gold leaf.

4. Roll bead on gold leaf. Try to cover as much of the bead as possible with the leaf. (There is no need to cover it entirely.) If necessary, use tweezers to press gold leaf gently onto bead.

TIP Applying gold leaf takes practice, so don't be frustrated if your first few attempts are less than perfect.

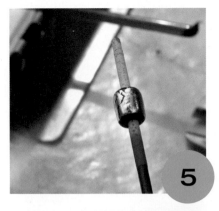

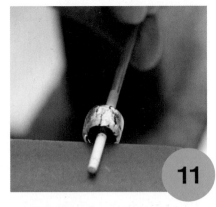

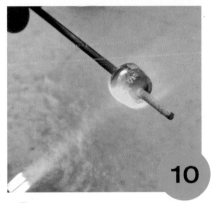

5. Heat bead very gently to fuse leaf onto bead.

TIP Gold leaf is delicate, and will burn away if too much heat is applied. Warm the bead with just enough heat so that cracks and fissures in the gold give the bead an intricate texture.

6. Keep bead warm, and heat transparent rod until there is a ball of very hot, very soft glass at tip.

7. Touch edge of molten ball to bead and wrap in a ring around bead.

TIP Work quickly when encasing gold leaf, so that the heat used to melt the transparent glass doesn't cause the gold leaf to burn off.

8. Flame-cut glass after first ring, then heat transparent rod until there is a ball of very hot, very soft molten glass at tip.

9. Repeat steps 7 and 8 until bead is completely encased in transparent glass. Ensure that rings overlap so no air trapped between rings.

10. Heat bead gently until surface is smooth.

11. Cool bead slightly; then roll gently on graphite paddle to shape a smooth cylinder. Roll top and bottom of bead against edge of graphite paddle to even up ends.

12. Heat bead gently until surface is smooth.

13. Move bead to edge of flame to cool until glow fades.

14. Sandwich bead between fiber blankets and set aside to cool completely.

Encased Filigrana Bead

Materials and Tools

- petroleum green glass rod
- transparent glass rod
- gold aventurine filigrana glass rod
- mandrel dipped in bead separator
- torch
- 2 fiber blankets

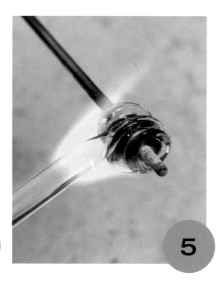

1. Wind a 16mm round bead (see steps 1 to 8, pages 16–17) with petroleum green glass.

2. Cool bead at edge of flame until firm.

3. Keep bead warm, and heat transparent rod until there is a ball of very hot, very soft molten glass at tip.

4. Touch edge of molten ball to bead and wrap in a ring around bead.

5. Continue heating transparent glass and wrapping rings around bead until bead is completely encased in transparent glass. Ensure that rings overlap so no air is trapped between rings.

6. Heat bead evenly until surface is smooth.

7. Cool bead slightly and heat tip of gold aventurine filigrana rod until molten.

TIP Heat filigrana rod at edge of flame. Take care not to overheat, since this glass is quite sensitive and tends to crack easily.

8. Touch molten tip at middle of bead and wrap a single ring around bead.

9. Heat bead evenly until surface is rounded and smooth.

10. Move bead to edge of flame to cool until glow fades.

11. Sandwich between fiber blankets and set aside to cool completely.

Aquatic Marine Necklace *(see page 98)*

Dotted Pressed Bead

Materials and Tools

- medium red glass rod
- straw yellow glass rod
- pea green glass rod
- medium red glass stringer (page 20)
- mandrel dipped in bead separator
- torch
- graphite paddle
- 2 fiber blankets

1. Wind a 20mm cylindrical bead (see steps 1 to 6, page 18) with medium red glass.

2. Cool bead at edge of flame until firm.

3. Keep bead warm, and heat straw yellow glass until there is a ball of very hot, very soft molten glass at tip.

4. Touch edge of molten ball to bead and wrap in a ring around bead.

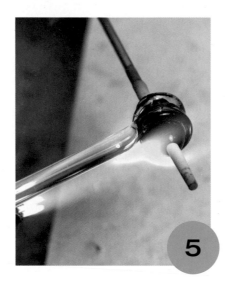

5. Continue heating straw yellow glass and wrapping rings around bead until bead is completely encased in straw yellow glass. Ensure that rings overlap so no air is trapped between rings.

6. Heat bead evenly until surface is smooth.

7. Cool bead slightly, then gently press one side of bead against graphite paddle to flatten.

8

11

14

8. Rotate bead 180 degrees and gently press on graphite paddle to flatten opposite side and form a lentil shape.

9. Heat bead gently until surface is smooth, and heat tip of pea green rod until molten.

10. Touch molten tip to middle of bead and make a dot.

11. Repeat step 10 to make a ring of dots around middle of bead.

12. Heat bead gently until dots are rounded but not absorbed. Heat tip of medium red stringer until molten.

13. Touch molten tip to one green dot to make a smaller red dot.

15

Candy Apple Earrings *(see page 88)*

14. Repeat step 13 to make smaller red dots on each green dot.

15. Heat bead gently until dots are rounded but not absorbed.

16. Move bead to edge of flame to cool until glow fades. Sandwich bead between fiber blankets and set aside to cool completely.

Encased Triangle Bead

Materials and Tools

- light blue glass rod
- white glass rod
- light sky blue glass rod
- cobalt blue glass rod
- transparent glass rod
- mandrel dipped in bead separator
- torch
- 2 fiber blankets

1. Wind an 18 mm round bead (see steps 1 to 8, pages 16–17) with light blue glass.

2. Cool bead at edge of flame until firm.

3. Keep bead warm, and heat tip of white rod until molten.

4. Touch molten tip at middle of bead and make a dot.

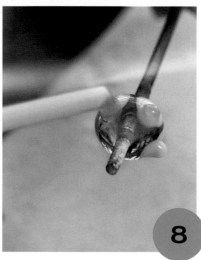

5. Repeat step 4 to make a ring of five evenly spaced dots around middle of bead.

6. Heat bead gently until dots are rounded but not absorbed. Heat tip of light sky blue glass rod until molten.

7. Touch molten tip at top of one white dot to make a dot that is partly on the white dot and partly on the base bead.

8. Repeat step 7 to make a ring of smaller dots at top of bead.

9. Heat bead gently until dots are rounded but not absorbed. Heat tip of cobalt blue glass rod until molten. (Heat the same amount of glass at the tip, since these dots should be similar to the light sky blue dots.)

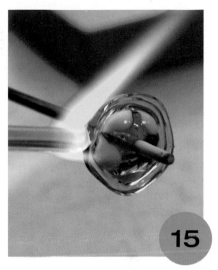

11

12

15

10. Touch molten tip at bottom of one the white dot to make a dot that is partly on white dot and partly on the base bead.

11. Repeat step 10 to make a ring of smaller dots at bottom of bead.

12. Heat bead evenly until dots are absorbed and surface is smooth.

13. Cool bead slightly and heat transparent rod until there is a ball of very hot, very soft molten glass at tip.

14. Touch edge of molten ball to middle of bead and wrap in a ring around bead.

15. Continue wrapping to make a second ring around center of bead. Ensure that rings overlap so no air is trapped between them. Do not wrap glass around top and bottom of bead.

16. Heat bead evenly until surface is rounded and smooth. Move bead to edge of flame to cool until glow fades. Sandwich between fiber blankets and set aside to cool completely.

Delicate Denim Pin *(see page 76)*

Tri-Color Cube Bead

Materials and Tools

- dark rose glass rod
- lavender glass rod
- transparent glass rod
- mandrel dipped in bead separator

- torch
- graphite paddle
- flattener
- 2 fiber blankets

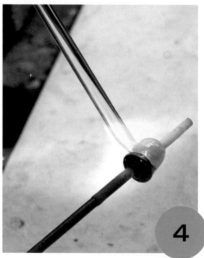

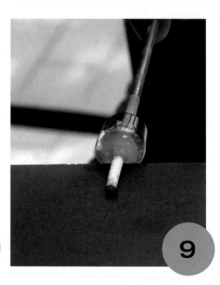

1. Wind an 8mm round bead (see steps 1 to 8, pages 16–17) with dark rose glass.

2. Keep bead warm, and heat tip of lavender rod until molten. Leave a space of about ¼" (6 mm) from first bead and wind a similar round lavender bead.

3. Keep beads warm and heat tip of transparent rod until molten.

4. Wind glass between beads to fill space completely, then heat beads until glass fuses to form a single bead.

5. Cool bead at edge of flame until firm. Keep bead warm, and heat transparent rod until there is a ball of very hot, very soft glass at tip.

6. Touch edge of the molten ball to bead and wrap a ring around bead.

7. Continue heating transparent glass and wrapping rings around bead until bead is completely encased in transparent glass. Ensure that rings overlap so no air is trapped between rings.

8. Heat bead evenly until surface is smooth.

9. Cool bead slightly, then roll top and bottom of bead against edge of graphite paddle to even up ends.

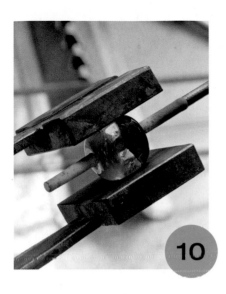

10

TIP If you don't have a flattener, simply press bead on marver or graphite paddle to flatten one side, then rotate bead 180 degrees and press to flatten other side. Rotate bead 90 degrees to flatten third side, then rotate again 180 degrees to flatten fourth side.

11. Heat bead gently until surface is smooth.

12. Move bead to edge of flame to cool until glow fades. Sandwich bead between fiber blankets and set aside to cool completely.

10. Place bead on one side of flattener and press gently to flatten. Rotate bead 90° and flatten other sides.

Lavender and Rose Cube Bracelet *(see page 104)*

Misted Cube Bead

Materials and Tools

- transparent glass rod
- dark rose glass rod
- mandrel dipped in bead separator
- torch
- graphite paddle
- 2 fiber blankets

1

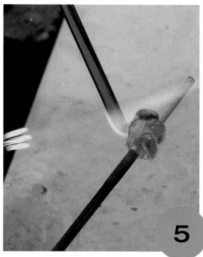

5

7

1. Wind an 8mm cylindrical bead (see steps 1 to 6, page 18) with transparent glass.

2. Cool bead at edge of flame until firm.

3. Keep bead warm, and heat tip of dark rose rod until molten.

4. Touch molten tip to bead and make a dot.

5. Repeat step 4 to make several more dots, as well as lines and other shapes, all over bead.

6. Keep bead warm, and heat tip of transparent glass rod.

7. Touch molten tip to bead and fill in spaces between dark rose decorations.

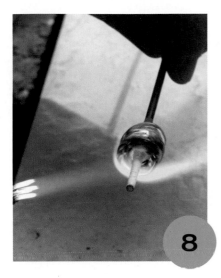

8. Heat bead gently until surface is smooth.

9. Cool bead slightly, then press gently on graphite paddle to flatten one side.

10. Rotate bead 180 degrees and flatten opposite side. Rotate bead 90 degrees and flatten. Rotate bead 180 degrees and flatten again.

TIP If you have a flattener, simply place bead on one side of it and press gently to flatten. Rotate bead 90 degrees and flatten other sides.

11. Roll top and bottom of bead against edge of graphite paddle to even up ends.

12. Heat bead evenly until surface is smooth. Move bead to edge of flame to cool until glow fades. Sandwich bead between fiber blankets and set aside to cool.

Feathered Bead

Materials and Tools

- transparent glass rod
- light turquoise stringer (page 20)
- mandrel dipped in bead separator
- torch
- graphite paddle
- sharp knife, set in a cup of water
- 2 fiber blankets

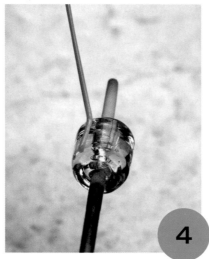

1. Wind an 8mm cylindrical bead (see steps 1 to 6, page 18) with transparent glass.

2. Cool bead at edge of flame until firm.

3. Keep bead warm, and heat tip of light turquoise stringer until molten.

4. Touch molten tip to one end of bead and draw a straight line to other end of bead.

5. Repeat step 4 to make evenly spaced lines all around bead.

6. Heat bead evenly until stripes are absorbed and surface is smooth.

9

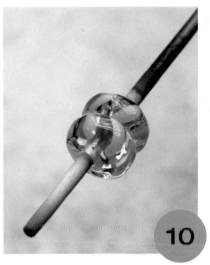

10

11

7. Cool bead slightly; then roll gently on graphite paddle to shape a smooth cylinder. Roll top and bottom of bead against edge of graphite paddle to even up ends.

8. Heat bead gently until surface is soft. Take care not to overheat as you want a firm core.

9. Press knife blade widthwise along middle of bead. Do not apply too much pressure, as you don't want blade to reach mandrel.

10. Rotate mandrel for one full twist while pressing in blade, to make a single continuous indent around middle of bead.

11. Heat bead evenly until indent vanishes and surface is smooth.

12. Move bead to edge of flame to cool until glow fades. Sandwich between fiber blankets and set aside to cool completely.

Beautiful Blue Eyes Bead

Materials and Tools

- light blue glass rod
- purple glass rod
- periwinkle glass rod

- light lapis glass rod
- rosato (blue pink) glass rod
- mandrel dipped in bead separator

- torch
- bead rake, set in a cup of water
- 2 fiber blankets

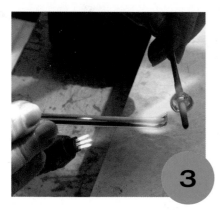

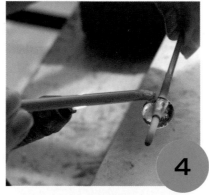

1. Wind a 15mm round bead (see steps 1 to 8, pages 16–17) with light blue glass.

2. Cool bead at edge of flame until firm.

3. Keep bead warm, and heat tip of purple rod until molten.

4. Touch molten tip at middle of bead and make a dot.

5. Repeat step 3 to make a ring of four evenly spaced dots around middle of bead.

6. Heat bead gently until dots are rounded but not absorbed. Heat tip of light lapis rod until molten.

7. Touch molten tip to bead and make a dot to one side of purple dots, and between every two dots.

8. Repeat step 7 to make a ring of evenly spaced light lapis dots on one side of purple dots. Be sure to place each light lapis dot between two purple dots.

9. Heat bead gently until dots are rounded but not absorbed. Heat tip of periwinkle rod until molten.

10. Touch molten tip to bead and make a dot on other side of purple dots, directly opposite a light lapis dot.

11. Repeat step 10 to make a ring of evenly spaced periwinkle dots on this end of bead.

12. Heat bead evenly until dots are absorbed and surface is smooth. Cool bead slightly.

13. Heat one purple dot until glowing, then plunge rake into center of dot to make a hole.

14. Repeat step 13 to make holes in every purple dot.

15. Keep bead warm, and heat tip of rosato rod to form a small ball of molten glass.

16. Touch molten tip to one hole to form a cap of glass over hole. (You want the glass to cover hole and trap air inside of it rather than fill the hole.)

17. Repeat step 16 to cover each hole with a cap of rosato glass.

18. Heat bead evenly until surface is smooth.

19. Move bead to edge of flame to cool until glow fades. Sandwich bead between fiber blankets and set aside to cool completely.

Transparent Flower Bead

Materials and Tools

- light teal glass rod
- jade green in clear filigrana glass rod
- light sky blue glass rod

- white glass stringer (page 20)
- light aquamarine glass rod
- mandrel dipped in bead separator

- torch
- bead rake, set in a cup of water
- 2 fiber blankets

1. Wind a 12mm round bead (see steps 1 to 8, pages 16–17) with light teal glass.

2. Cool bead at edge of flame until firm.

3. Keep bead warm, and heat tip of jade green in clear filigrana rod until molten.

TIP Heat filigrana rod at edge of flame. Take care not to overheat, since this glass is quite sensitive and tends to crack easily.

4. Touch molten tip at one end of bead, and draw a diagonal line to other end of bead. Switch directions and draw a diagonal line back to other end of bead.

5. Continue in this manner to make a zigzag all around bead. Be sure to end zigzag where it started.

6. Heat bead evenly until zigzag is absorbed and surface is smooth.

7. Cool bead slightly and heat the tip of light sky blue glass rod until molten.

8. Touch molten tip near middle of bead and make a dot.

9. Repeat step 8 to make three more dots, close together but not touching, to form a cluster of dots around middle of bead.

10. Repeat steps 8 and 9 to make four more evenly spaced clusters of dots around middle of bead.

11

17

23

12

25

11. Heat bead evenly until dots are absorbed and surface is smooth. Heat tip of light aquamarine rod until molten. (Heat a smaller part of tip than you did in step 7 because you want these dots to be smaller.)

12. Touch molten tip to one light blue dot to make a smaller light aquamarine dot.

13. Repeat step 12 to make smaller light aquamarine dots on each light blue dot.

14. Heat bead evenly until dots are absorbed and surface is smooth. Heat tip of white stringer until molten.

15. Touch molten tip in center of a cluster and make a dot.

16. Repeat step 15 to make two more dots, close together but not touching, to form a triangle of dots in the center of the cluster.

17. Repeat steps 15 and 16 to make a triangle of white dots in the center of each cluster.

18. Heat bead gently until dots are rounded but not absorbed. Heat tip of light aquamarine rod until molten.

19. Touch molten tip to one white dot to make a smaller light aquamarine dot.

20. Repeat step 19 to make smaller light aquamarine dots on each white dot.

21. Heat bead evenly until dots are absorbed and surface is smooth. Cool bead slightly.

22. Heat one cluster of dots until glowing, then plunge bead rake into center of cluster to make a hole.

23. Repeat step 22 to make holes in center of every cluster. Keep bead warm, and heat tip of light aquamarine rod to form a small ball of molten glass.

24. Touch molten tip to one hole to form a cap of glass over hole. (You want the glass to cover hole and trap air inside of it rather than fill the hole.)

25. Repeat step 24 to cover each hole with a cap of light aquamarine glass. Heat bead evenly until surface is smooth.

26. Move bead to edge of flame to cool until glow fades. Sandwich bead between fiber blankets and set aside to cool.

Textured Leaf Bead

Materials and Tools

- light grass green rod
- mandrel dipped in bead separator
- torch
- leaf masher

- 2 fiber blankets
- gold leaf
- marver
- tweezers

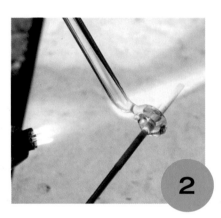

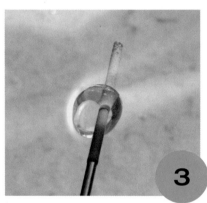

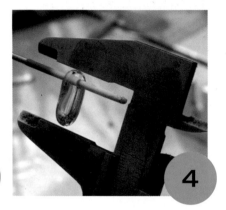

1. Wind an 8mm round bead (see steps 1 to 8, pages 16–17) with light grass green glass.

2. Continue winding bead, allowing more glass to build up one side of the bead.

3. Stop rotating bead for a moment to allow molten glass to be drawn downward with gravity.

TIP To make several beads of the same length, measure beads with a caliper as you work.

4. Continue heating glass rod while rotating bead to increase bead size. Pause periodically while rotating to allow glass to build up on one side, until bead is desired size. Take care area of bead along top of mandrel isn't too thin, as this can cause bead to crack later.

5. Cool bead slightly, then bring leaf masher to bead and press once gently.

TIP Take care not to press bead with leaf masher for too long, as this causes surface of bead to cool, and could lead to thermal shock.

6. Heat bead very gently until surface is smooth. Take care not to overheat as this will cause imprint to disappear.

7. Move bead to edge of flame to cool until glow fades. Sandwich bead between fiber blankets and set aside to cool completely.

Adding Gold Leaf

1. Lay gold leaf on marver before winding bead, and keep marver close at hand.

2. Follow steps 1 to 6 (above). Touch bead to gold leaf and press gently to affix, or use tweezers to grasp gold leaf and bring it to hot bead.

TIP Gold leaf is delicate and will burn away if too much heat is applied. Warm the bead with just enough heat so that cracks and fissures in the gold give the bead an interesting, intricate texture.

3. Heat bead very gently to fuse leaf onto bead.

4. Move bead to edge of flame to cool until glow fades. Sandwich bead between fiber blankets and set aside to cool completely.

Swirled Stripe Bead

Materials and Tools

- medium grass green glass rod
- powder pink glass stringer (page 20)
- mandrel dipped in bead separator
- torch
- graphite paddle
- 2 fiber blankets

1

5

6

1. Wind a 12mm cylindrical bead (see steps 1 to 6, page 18) with medium grass green glass.

2. Cool bead at edge of flame until firm.

3. Keep bead warm, and heat tip of medium grass green glass until molten.

4. Touch molten tip near one end of bead and make a dot.

5. Repeat step 4 to make a ring of four evenly spaced dots at this end of bead.

6. Make a similar ring of dots at other end of bead. Each dot at this end should be directly opposite the spaces between dots in first ring.

7. Cool bead slightly and heat tip of powder pink stringer until molten.

8. Touch molten tip to middle of bead, in space between rings of dots, and wrap around middle of bead, guided by contours of the dots, to form a wavy strip.

9. Heat bead evenly until dots and line are absorbed and surface is smooth.

10. Move bead to edge of flame to cool until glow fades. Sandwich bead between fiber blankets and set aside to cool.

Swirls of Twirls Necklace *(see page 116)*

Twisted Swirl Bead

Materials and Tools

- transparent glass rod
- light turquoise glass rod
- mandrel dipped in bead separator
- torch
- graphite paddle
- 2 fiber blankets

1

4

6

1. Wind an 8mm cylindrical bead (see steps 1 to 6, page 18) with transparent glass.

2. Cool bead at edge of flame until firm.

3. Keep bead warm, and heat tip of light turquoise rod until molten.

4. Touch molten tip at one end of bead and draw a diagonal line to other end of bead.

5. Rotate bead 180 degrees and make another diagonal line, from one end of bead to other.

6. Rotate bead 90 degrees and repeat steps 4 and 5 to make a total of four evenly spaced diagonal lines.

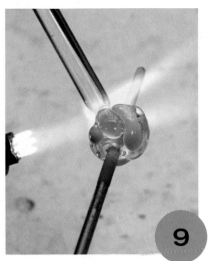

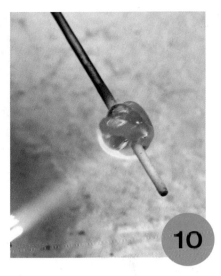

7. Cool bead slightly and heat tip of transparent rod until molten.

8. Touch molten tip at one end of bead, between two turquoise lines, and draw in a diagonal line to other end.

9. Repeat step 8 another three times to fill spaces between all turquoise lines with lines of transparent glass.

10. Heat bead evenly until surface is smooth.

11. Move bead to edge of flame to cool until the glow fades. Sandwich bead between fiber blankets and set aside to cool completely.

Surreal Sky Necklace *(see page 83)*

Powdered Enamel Bead

Materials and Tools

- burgundy enamel powder
- mustard enamel powder
- dark ivory glass rod

- marver
- tweezers
- graphite paddle

- mandrel dipped in bead separator
- torch
- 2 fiber blankets

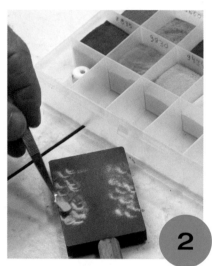

1. Sprinkle burgundy enamel powder on marver. Use tweezers to distribute enamel powder evenly, and cover an area that is about three times as wide as desired bead.

2. Sprinkle mustard enamel powder on top of burgundy enamel powder and distribute evenly. Use tweezers to press enamel powder onto marver.

3. Wind a 12mm bicone bead (see steps 1 to 8, page 19) with dark ivory glass.

4. Cool bead at edge of flame until firm.

5. Heat one end of bead until glowing.

6

8

11

6. Lay glowing end on edge of enamel powder and roll in enamel until covered.

7. Heat this end of bead very gently until surface is smooth.

TIP You'll need a bicone bead to pick up the enamel powder when building this bead. Since you'll be shaping it into a round bead during the final heating, don't worry if the bicone bead isn't perfectly symmetrical.

10

12

8. Heat other end of bead until glowing, and repeat steps 6 and 7.

9. Heat this end of bead very gently until surface is smooth.

10. Heat middle of bead until glowing, then roll in remaining enamel powder.

11. Heat bead gently until bead is rounded and surface is smooth.

12. Move bead to edge of flame to cool until glow fades. Sandwich between fiber blankets and set aside to cool completely.

Scaled Bead

Materials and Tools

- light grass green glass rod
- white glass rod
- gold pink striking glass rod
- medium grass green glass rod

- mandrel dipped in bead separator
- torch
- 2 fiber blankets

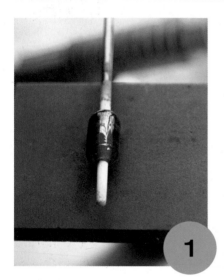

1

5

6

1. Wind a 12mm cylindrical bead (see steps 1 to 6, page 18) with light green glass.

2. Cool bead at edge of flame until firm.

3. Keep bead warm, and heat tip of white rod until molten.

4. Touch molten tip near one end of bead and make a small dot.

5. Repeat step 4 to make a ring of evenly spaced dots at this end of bead. Take care that the dots are close together but not touching.

6. Heat bead evenly until dots are absorbed and surface is smooth.

7. Cool bead slightly and heat tip of gold pink striking rod until molten.

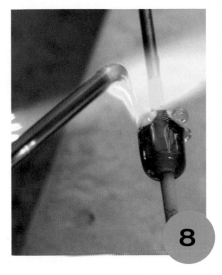

8. Touch molten tip to one white dot to make a dot that is partly on white dot and partly on base bead. Be sure that a crescent-shaped sliver of white dot remains visible.

9. Repeat step 8 to place gold pink striking dots on each white dot.

10. Heat bead evenly until dots are absorbed and surface is smooth.

11. Cool bead slightly and heat tip of white rod until molten.

12. Touch molten tip to bead and make a dot that is partly on first ring of dots and partly on base bead. Dot should be placed between two dots in first ring, slightly overlapping both dots.

13. Repeat step 12 to make a ring of dots that overlaps first ring of dots.

14. Heat bead until dots are absorbed and surface is smooth.*

15. Cool bead slightly and heat tip of gold pink striking rod until molten.

16. Repeat steps 8 to 14 until most of bead is covered with rings of white and gold pink striking dots. When there is room for just two more rings of dots, replace gold pink striking rod with medium grass green rod, and make final two rings of dots with green glass.

17. Heat bead gently until surface is smooth. Move bead to edge of flame to cool until glow fades. Sandwich bead between fiber blankets and set aside to cool completely.

* To form a pear-shaped bead, allow bead to swell naturally with every ring of dots. To form a cylindrical bead, roll bead gently on graphite paddle after each ring of dots is added.

Protruding Flower Bead

Materials and Tools

- opaque turquoise glass rod
- white glass rod
- transparent pink glass rod
- transparent green glass rod
- opaque orange glass rod
- mandrel dipped in bead separator
- torch
- sharp knife, set in a cup of water
- 2 fiber blankets

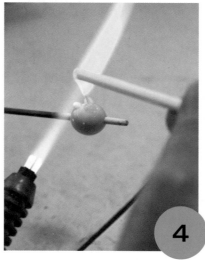

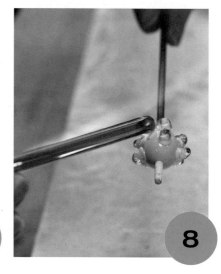

1. Wind a 12mm round bead (see steps 1 to 8, pages 16–17) with opaque turquoise glass.

2. Cool bead at edge of flame until firm.

3. Keep bead warm, and heat tip of ivory rod until molten.

4. Touch molten tip to middle of bead and make a dot.

5. Repeat step 4 to make two more dots, close together but not touching, to form a triangle of dots clustered around middle of bead.

6. Repeat steps 4 and 5 to make two more evenly spaced triangles of dots around middle of bead.

7. Heat bead gently until dots are rounded but not absorbed. Heat tip of transparent pink rod until molten.

8. Touch molten tip to one white dot to make a transparent pink dot.

9. Repeat step 8 to make transparent pink dots on each white dot.

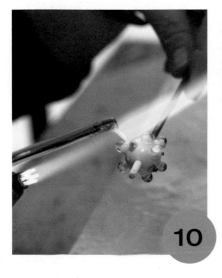

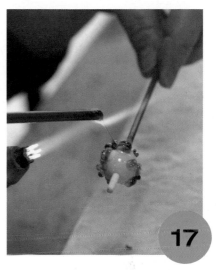

10. Heat bead gently until dots are rounded but not absorbed. Heat tip of transparent green rod until molten.

11. Touch molten tip on both sides of each dot cluster and make two dots that frame each cluster. Heat bead gently until dots are rounded but not absorbed.

12. Heat a cluster of dots until glowing, then draw knife through each dot in cluster, from the center outward, to form petals.

13. Repeat step 12 to make flowers out of every cluster.

14. Heat a green dot until glowing, then draw knife through dot, from the center outward, to form a leaf.

15. Repeat step 14 to make leaves on both sides of every cluster.

16. Heat tip of opaque orange rod until molten.

17. Touch middle of each flower with molten tip.

18. Heat bead evenly until dots are rounded but not absorbed.

19. Move bead to edge of flame to cool until glow fades. Sandwich bead between fiber blankets and set aside to cool.

Part 2:
Glass Bead Jewelry

Useful Tips

- Before stringing your design, arrange beads on a soft, neutral-colored fabric (a white or beige towel is perfect). This gives you a chance to adjust the order of the beads according to your particular taste.

- When making symmetrical necklaces or bracelets, it's best to string center beads first and then add beads on either side. If the project requires relatively few beads, you may find it easier to finish one side first and then move to the other. If the project involves many beads and several stringing patterns, it may be easier to move from one side of the necklace or bracelet to the other, gradually building up both sides at the same time.

- Many photographs in the following pages are detail photographs. They only include the beads discussed in a particular step in order to illustrate that step as clearly as possible.

- All lengths of bead cord and wire are generous estimates. Please measure and adjust accordingly.

- It may be difficult to find the exact size, shape, and color of the beads used in these projects. This is particularly true of the crystal beads, which manufacturers label in different ways. Use the descriptions in these projects as guidelines, and choose whichever beads catch your eye, capture your imagination, and complement your handmade beads.

- Use wire-cutters to trim head pins and eye pins after decorating them with beads. Use round-nose pliers to make a loop at the end of the pin. This loop secures the beads on the pins and enables you to string the pins in your project.

Golden Leaf Choker

Show off a single stunning bead with this project.

Materials and Tools

- one 19mm handmade encased gold leaf bead (page 34), gold and red, cylindrical, with large round hole
- two 4mm antique gold rondelle beads
- two 9mm antique gold barrel beads, with large holes
- two 4mm antique gold crimp tubes with loop, with large holes
- two 6mm antique gold jump rings.
- one antique gold clasp
- one piece ⅛" (4 mm) piece of blue silicon beading cord, 18" (46 cm) long
- wire cutters
- flat-nose pliers

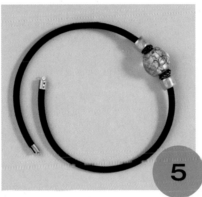

6. Open a jump ring and string through loop on one crimp tube. String clasp onto jump ring and close jump ring.

7. Open other jump ring and string through ring on other crimp tube. Close jump ring.

1. String handmade encased gold leaf bead onto cord and draw to middle of cord.

2. Work on one side of necklace: string one rondelle bead and one barrel bead onto cord.

3. Repeat step 2 on other side of necklace.

4. Work on one side of necklace: place one crimp tube at end of cord and flatten.

5. Repeat step 4 on other side of necklace.

Strawberries in Spring Necklace

Like a bowl of freshly picked strawberries, this necklace is sweet and refreshing.

Materials and Tools

- three handmade scaled beads (page 60), in the following colors and sizes:
  - one 25mm pink and green, round
  - two 25mm pink and green, pear-shaped
- two 25mm handmade dotted sandwich beads (page 22), pink and green
- twenty-two 3mm sky blue seed beads
- four 5mm sky blue glass beads
- twenty-four 3mm matte turquoise seed beads
- twenty-four 3mm glossy light green seed beads
- twelve 3mm transparent light green seed beads
- eight 3mm glossy petroleum green seed beads
- six 3mm glossy fuchsia seed beads
- two silver crimp beads
- two silver jump rings
- one silver clasp
- two 20" (51 cm) 18-gauge silver-filled half-hard wires
- flat-nose pliers
- wire cutters

1. Hold wires together and string round handmade scaled bead onto both wires. Draw bead to middle of wires.

2. Work on one side of necklace: hold wires apart and string one sky blue seed bead on each wire. Hold wires together and string one sky blue glass bead on both wires.

3. Hold wires together and string one pear-shaped handmade scaled bead on both wires, orienting bead so that pink end faces middle of necklace.

4. Repeat steps 2 and 3 on other side of necklace.

(continued)

5. Work on one side of necklace: hold wires apart and string one turquoise seed bead on each wire. Hold wires together and string one handmade dotted sandwich bead on both wires, orienting bead so that green end faces middle of necklace. Hold wires apart and string two turquoise seed beads on each wire.

6. Repeat step 5 on other side of necklace.

7. Work on one side of necklace: hold wires together and string beads in the following order: one sky blue glass bead, one transparent light green seed bead, one petroleum green seed bead, one fuchsia seed bead, one petroleum green seed bead, one transparent light green seed bead, three sky blue seed beads, and three turquoise seed beads.

8. On same side of necklace, string one transparent light green seed bead, one petroleum green seed bead, one fuchsia seed bead, one petroleum green seed bead, one transparent light green seed bead, three sky blue seed beads, and three turquoise seed beads.

9. On same side of necklace, string six glossy light green seed beads, one turquoise seed bead, one sky blue seed bead, one transparent light green seed bead, one fuchsia seed bead, one transparent light green seed bead, one sky blue seed bead, one turquoise seed bead, and six glossy light green seed beads.

10. Hold wires together and string one crimp bead, drawing it along until it is flush with other beads. Make a loop in wires and draw ends back through crimp bead. Flatten crimp bead and trim wires.

11. Open a jump ring and string through loop. String half of clasp onto jump ring and close jump ring.

12. Repeat steps 5 to 10 on other side of necklace. Open other jump ring and string through loop. String other half of clasp through jump ring and close jump ring.

Garden Necklace

Have a fresh bouquet in every season with this flowery necklace.

Materials and Tools

- nine handmade protruding flower beads (page 62), in the following colors and sizes:
  - one 17mm sky blue with pink and green, round
  - eight 15mm sky blue with pink and green, round
- four 8mm handmade flush dotted beads (page 21), sky blue with pink, round
- thirty-four 3mm turquoise seed bead
- eight 5mm sky blue glass beads, round

- twenty-six 3mm transparent light green seed beads
- twenty 3mm sky blue seed beads
- four 3mm fuchsia seed beads
- two gold jump rings
- two gold crimp beads
- one gold clasp
- two 22" (56 cm) 24-gauge gold-filled nylon wires
- flat-nose pliers
- wire cutters

1. Hold wires together and string largest handmade protruding flower bead onto both wires. Draw bead to middle of wires.

2. Work on one side of necklace: hold wires apart and string one turquoise seed bead on each wire. Hold wires together and string one sky blue glass bead, one smaller handmade protruding flower bead, one turquoise seed bead, and one smaller handmade protruding flower bead.

3. Hold wires apart and string one turquoise seed bead and one transparent light green seed bead on each wire. Hold wires together and string one smaller protruding flower bead on both wires. Hold wires apart and string one turquoise seed bead and one transparent light green seed bead on each wire.

4. Hold wires together and string one protruding flower bead, one sky blue glass bead, one handmade flush dotted bead, one sky blue glass bead, one handmade flush dotted bead, and one sky blue glass bead on both wires.

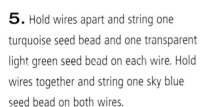
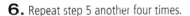

5 (image label)

7 (image label)

9 (image label)

5. Hold wires apart and string one turquoise seed bead and one transparent light green seed bead on each wire. Hold wires together and string one sky blue seed bead on both wires.

6. Repeat step 5 another four times.

7. Hold wires together and string three turquoise seed beads, two transparent light green seed beads, one fuchsia bead, three sky blue seed beads, one fuchsia seed bead, two transparent light green seed beads, three turquoise seed beads, and one sky blue seed bead.

8. Hold wires together and string one crimp bead onto both wires. Make a loop in wires and draw ends back through crimp bead. Flatten crimp bead and trim wires.

9. Open a jump ring and string through loop. String clasp onto jump ring and close jump ring.

10. Repeat steps 2 to 8 on other side of necklace. Open other jump ring, string through loop, and close jump ring.

Delicate Denim Pin

This denim-colored pin matches perfectly with
your favorite pair of blue jeans.

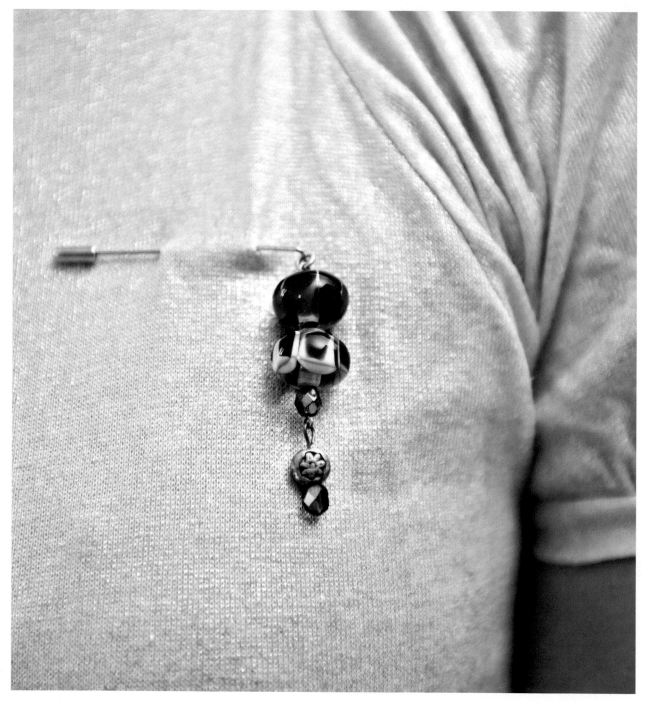

Materials and Tools

- two 13mm handmade encased triangle beads (page 40), blue and white
- two 6mm sapphire crystal beads, faceted round
- one 18mm silver flat flower bead
- one silver jump ring
- one 1⅜" (3.5 cm) silver stick pin with loop
- one silver head pin
- one silver eye pin

- wire cutters
- round-nose pliers

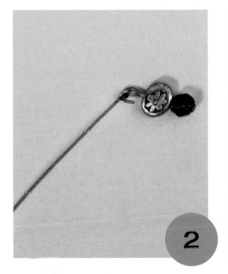

1. String one crystal bead and flat flower bead onto head pin. Trim head pin and form a loop.

2. String loop in head pin through loop in eye pin and close loop.

3. String one crystal bead and both encased triangle beads onto eye pin.

4. Trim eye pin and form a loop. Open a jump ring, string through loop, and close loop.

5. Open stick pin, string jump ring with decorated eye pin, and close stick pin.

Charming Elephant
Charm Necklace

Simple to make, this pendant makes a big impression.

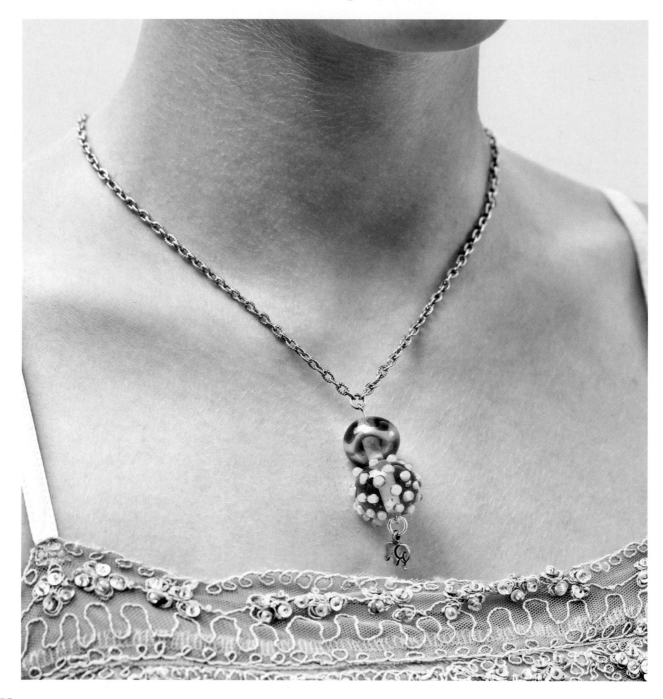

Materials and Tools

- one 47mm handmade porcupine bead (page 21), amber and yellow, round
- one 15mm handmade swirled stripe bead (page 54), amber and yellow, round
- one silver elephant charm
- two silver jump rings
- one silver eye pin
- 35" (89 cm) of silver link chain
- wire cutters
- round-nose pliers

1. Open a jump ring and string on elephant charm. String jump ring through loop in eye pin and close jump ring.

2. String handmade porcupine bead and swirled stripe bead onto eye pin. Trim eye pin and form a loop.

3. Open other jump ring and string through top loop in eye pin. String both ends of chain through jump ring and close jump ring.

Bumblebee and Rock Necklace

The handmade beads in this necklace are made from flat glass, but you'd never know it from the funky rocky shapes.

Materials and Tools

- eleven 15mm handmade rocky beads (page 26), various colors and shapes
- 10 g of 3mm yellow and black striped seed beads
- sixteen 6mm silver disk beads
- two 10mm silver cylindrical beads
- two silver crimp beads
- one silver bird-shaped clasp
- two silver jump rings
- three pieces 22" (56 cm) 18-gauge gold-filled half-hard wires

- flat-nose pliers
- wire cutters

1. Decide order of handmade rocky beads before stringing necklace. Hold wires together and string middle rocky bead on all three wires. Draw bead to middle of wires.

2. Work on one side of necklace: hold wires apart and string one seed bead on each wire.

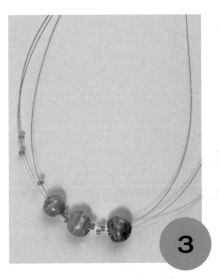

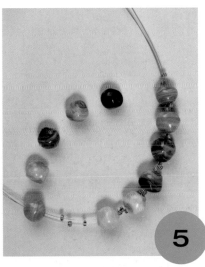

3. Hold wires together and string one rocky bead on all three wires. Hold wires apart and string one seed bead on each wire.

4. Repeat step 3 another four times.

5. Repeat steps 2 to 4 on other side of necklace.

6. Work on one side of necklace: hold wires together and string one silver disk bead onto all three wires. Hold wires apart and string six seed beads onto each wire.

(continued)

7. Repeat step 6 another five times.

8. Hold wires together and string one disk bead, one cylindrical bead, one disk bead, and one crimp bead onto all three wires. Draw crimp bead along wires until it is flush with other beads. Make a loop in wires and draw ends back through crimp bead. Flatten crimp bead and trim wires.

9. Open a jump ring and string into loop. String half of clasp onto jump ring and close jump ring.

10. Repeat steps 2 to 9 on other side of necklace. Open other jump ring and string into loop. String other half of clasp onto jump ring and close jump ring.

Surreal Sky Necklace

This elegant necklace features a variety of
handmade beads. Their delicate light colors
create an unearthly effect.

Materials and Tools

- seven large round handmade beads, in the following sizes and colors:
  - three 15mm feathered beads (page 46), pale blue with light sky blue, round
  - two 15mm flush dotted beads (page 21), pale blue with light sky blue, round
  - two 15mm twisted swirl beads (page 56), pale blue with light sky blue, round
- two 8mm handmade beads (page 16), light sky blue, round
- two 7mm handmade flush dotted beads (page 21), pale blue and light sky blue dots, round

- two 9 x 18mm handmade textured beads (page 27), pale blue and light sky blue, cylindrical
- fifty 5mm sky blue glass beads
- four 5 x 12mm silver cylindrical beads
- twenty-four 5mm silver disk beads
- two silver crimp beads
- one silver clasp
- two silver jump rings
- two 22" (56 cm) 18-gauge silver-filled nylon wires
- flat-nose pliers
- wire cutters

1. Decide order of large round handmade beads (feathered, flush dotted, and twisted swirl) before stringing necklace. You'll need five beads for middle of necklace, and one on each end. Hold wires together and string middle large round handmade bead on both wires. Draw bead to middle of wires.

2. Work on one side of necklace: hold wires apart and string one sky blue glass bead on each wire separately. Hold wires together and string one large round handmade bead on both wires.

3. Repeat step 2 one time.

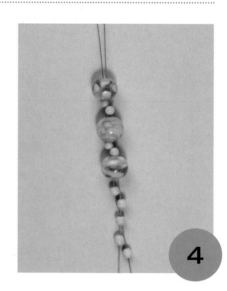

4

4. Hold wires together and string one sky blue glass bead on both wires. Hold wires apart and string one sky blue glass bead on each wire. Hold wires together and string one sky blue glass bead on both wires. Hold wires apart and string one sky blue glass bead on each wire.

5. Repeat steps 2 to 4 on other side of necklace.

6. Work on one side of necklace: hold wires together and string one large handmade bead, one silver disk bead, one small round handmade bead, one silver disk bead, one handmade flush dotted bead, one silver disk bead, and one textured bead on both wires.

7. Repeat step 6 on other side of necklace.

8. Work on one side of necklace: hold wires together and string one silver disk bead, one sky blue glass bead, one silver disk bead, one silver cylindrical bead, one silver disk bead, and one sky blue glass bead on both wires.

9. Repeat step 8 one time.

10. Hold wires together and string one silver disk bead, one sky blue glass bead, one silver disk bead, one sky blue glass bead, one silver disk bead, five sky blue glass beads, one silver disk bead, five sky blue glass beads, one silver cylindrical bead, and one silver disk bead.

11. String one crimp bead, drawing it along until it is flush with other beads. Make a loop in wires and draw ends back through crimp bead. Flatten crimp bead and trim wires.

12. Open a jump ring and string through loop. String half of clasp onto jump ring and close jump ring.

13. Repeat steps 8 to 11 on other side of necklace. Open other jump ring and string through loop. String other half of clasp onto jump ring and close jump ring.

Stellar Earrings

These earrings are out of sight...and so easy to make.

Materials and Tools

- two 18 x 13mm handmade dotted disk beads (page 24), blue and red
- two 3mm gold double-disk beads
- two 3mm gold round beads
- pair of gold hoop earrings
- glue

1. Open one gold hoop earring and string one double-disk bead, one handmade dotted disk bead, and one gold round bead.

2. Position beads near middle of hoop. (Hold up to your ear to check exact position).

3. Place a drop of glue on beads to secure.

4. Repeat steps 1 to 3 to make second earring.

Candy Apple Earrings

These earrings are simple and sweet.

Materials and Tools

- two 13 x 22mm handmade dotted pressed beads (page 38), red with green and red
- two 3mm light green seed beads
- two 3mm red seed beads
- two gold head pins
- pair of gold lever-back ear wires with loop

- wire cutters
- round-nose pliers

1. String one light green seed bead, one handmade dotted pressed bead, and one red seed bead onto a head pin.

2. Trim head pin and form a loop.

3. Open loop in one ear wire and string it through loop in head pin. Close loop in ear wire.

4. Repeat steps 1 to 3 to make second earring.

Hanging Garden Earrings

The beads in these distinct earrings are the signature
of an experienced glass bead maker. Once you've
mastered the technique, you'll want everyone to know.

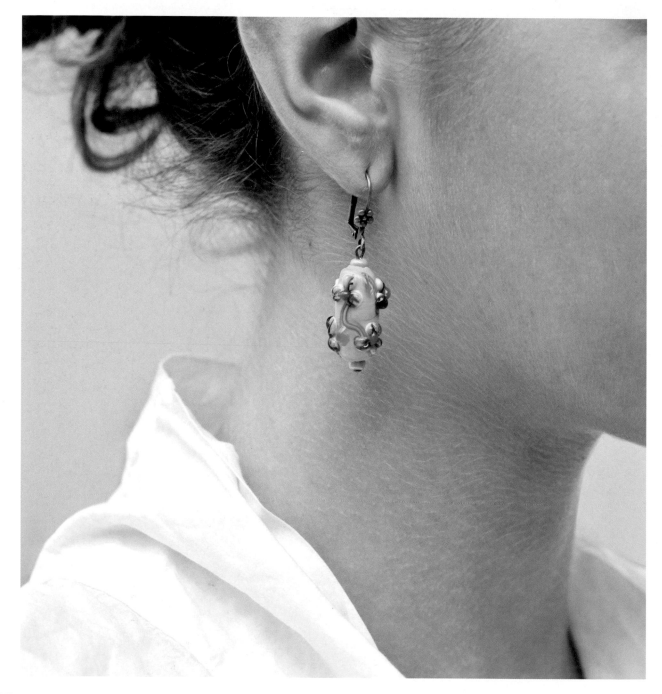

Materials and Tools

- two 13 x 20mm handmade protruding flower beads (page 62), light green with green and pink, cylindrical
- four 3mm light green seed beads
- two gold head pins

- pair of gold lever-back ear wires with loop

1. String one light green seed bead, one handmade protruding flower bead, and one light green seed bead onto a head pin.

2. Trim head pin and form a loop.

3. Open loop in one ear wire and string it through loop in head pin. Close loop in ear wire.

4. Repeat steps 1 to 3 to make second earring.

Autumn Fire Necklace

With a hint of gold leaf in these handmade beads
and an assortment of metallic gold beads, this
necklace is simply regal.

Materials and Tools

- three handmade encased gold leaf beads (page 34), in the following colors and sizes:
    - one 15 x 25mm red striking, cylindrical
    - two 13 x 14mm red striking, cylindrical
- twenty-four 3mm antique gold seed beads
- eight 4mm red crystal beads, faceted rondelle
- twelve 5mm amber with gold core crystal beads, faceted round
- twelve 5mm transparent yellow crystal beads, faceted round
- forty 3mm transparent amber glass beads, round
- two gold crimp beads
- two antique gold jump rings
- one antique gold clasp
- two 22" (56 cm) 18-gauge gold-filled half-hard wires
- flat-nose pliers
- wire cutters

1. Hold wires together and string largest handmade encased gold leaf bead onto both wires. Draw bead to middle of wires.

2. Work on one side of necklace: hold wires apart and string one antique gold seed bead on each wire separately. Hold wires together and string one small handmade encased gold leaf bead onto both wires. Hold wires apart and string one antique gold seed bead onto each wire.

3. Repeat step 2 on other side of necklace.

(continued)

Glass Bead Jewelry **93**

4

6. Hold wires together and string three transparent yellow crystal beads, one red crystal bead, one antique gold seed bead, one red crystal bead, one antique gold seed bead, and one red crystal bead on both wires.

7. String three amber with gold core crystal beads and ten transparent amber glass beads.

8. Repeat step 7, then string one crimp bead onto both wires and draw along until it is flush with other beads. Make a loop in wires and draw ends back through crimp bead. Flatten crimp bead and trim wires.

9

9. Open a jump ring and string through loop. String half of clasp onto jump ring and close jump ring.

10. Repeat steps 4 to 9 on other side of necklace. Open other jump ring and string through loop. String other half of clasp onto jump ring and close jump ring.

4. Work on one side of necklace: hold wires together and string one transparent yellow crystal bead on both wires.

5. Hold wires apart and string one antique gold seed bead on each wire separately. Hold wires together and string one red crystal bead on both wires. Hold wires apart and string one antique gold seed bead on each wire separately.

Bold Beaded Ball Necklace

This striking necklace requires basic round
handmade beads. A perfect first project.

Materials and Tools

- eleven 20mm handmade round beads (page 16), various colors
- thirty-four 3mm antique gold seed beads
- six 14mm orange and amber round agate beads
- seventeen gold eye pins
- one 4" (20 cm) antique gold chain, consisting of sixteen links that can be opened
- two antique gold jump rings
- one antique gold clasp

- wire cutters
- round-nose pliers

1. String one antique gold seed bead, one handmade round bead, and one antique gold seed bead onto an eye pin. Trim eye pin and form a loop.

2. Repeat step 1 another ten times.

3. String one antique gold seed bead, one agate bead, and one antique gold seed bead onto an eye pin. Trim eye pin and form a loop.

4. Repeat step 3 another five times.

5. Open all chain links.

6. Arrange decorated eye pins end-to-end on work surface. Place eye pins with handmade beads in middle of necklace, and three eye pins with agate beads at either end.

7. Draw an open chain link through loops in adjacent decorated eye pins. Close link to secure eye pins together.

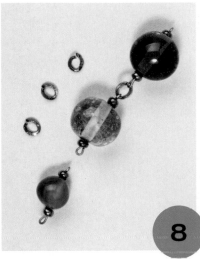

8. Repeat step 7 to attach all decorated eye pins in a single line.

9. Open a jump ring and string through loop at one end of necklace. String clasp through jump ring and close jump ring.

10. Open other jump ring and string through loop at other end of necklace.

Aquatic Marine Necklace

With watery blues and grassy greens, this necklace creates a stunning, yet soothing effect.

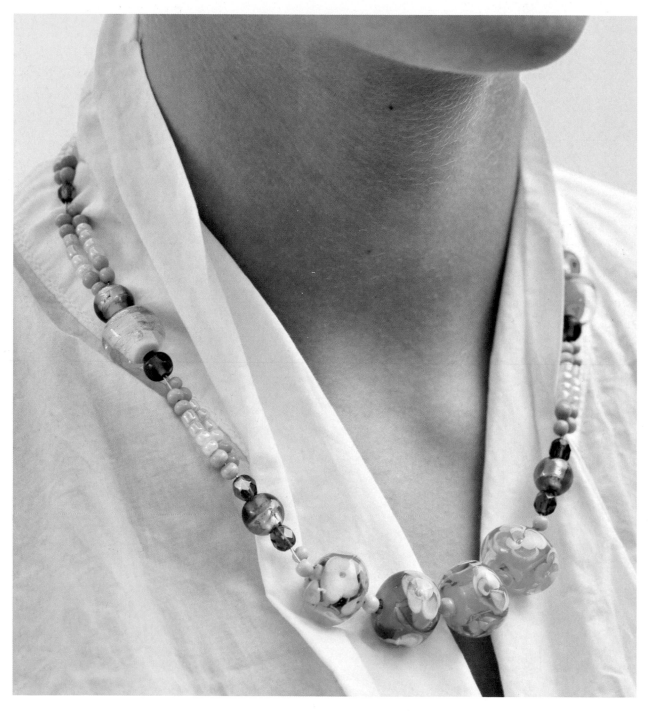

Materials and Tools

- four 15mm handmade transparent flower beads (page 50), turquoise, green, and white, round
- two 17mm handmade encased filigrana beads (page 36), round
  – one green with transparent and gold aventurine
  – one sky blue with transparent and gold aventurine
- fifty-eight 4mm sky blue glass beads, round
- ten 6mm turquoise crystal beads, faceted round
- four 10mm metallic green and turquoise glass beads, round
- sixty-four 3mm glossy light green seed beads
- two 6mm dotted antique gold beads, round
- two gold crimp beads
- two gold jump rings
- one antique gold clasp
- two 22" (56 cm) 18-gauge gold-filled half-hard wires
- flat-nose pliers
- wire cutters

1. Decide order of handmade transparent flower beads before stringing necklace. Hold wires together and string one of two middle transparent flower beads onto both wires. Draw bead to middle of wires.

2. Hold wires apart and string one sky blue glass bead on each wire. Hold wires together and string second middle transparent flower beads onto both wires.

3. Work on one side of necklace: hold wires apart and string one sky blue glass bead on each wire. Hold wires together and string one handmade flower bead on both wires. Hold wires apart and string one sky blue bead on each wire.

4. Repeat step 3 on other side of necklace.

(continued)

5. Work on one side of necklace: hold wires together and string one turquoise crystal bead, one metallic green and turquoise bead, and one turquoise crystal bead on both wires.

6. Hold wires apart and two sky blue glass beads, four glossy light green seed beads, and two sky blue glass beads on each wire separately.

7. Hold wires together and string one turquoise crystal bead, one handmade encased filigrana bead, and one metallic green and turquoise bead on both wires.

8. Repeat step 6, then string one turquoise crystal bead.

9. Hold wires apart and string two sky blue glass beads, twelve glossy light green seed beads, and two sky blue glass beads on each wire.

10. Hold wires together and string one turquoise crystal bead and one dotted antique gold bead onto both wires. String one crimp bead and draw it along until it is flush with the other beads. Make a loop in wires and draw ends back through crimp bead. Flatten crimp bead and trim wires.

11. Open a jump ring and string through loop. String half of clasp onto jump ring and close jump ring.

12. Repeat steps 5 to 10 on other side of necklace. Open other jump ring and string through loop. String other half of clasp onto jump ring and close jump ring.

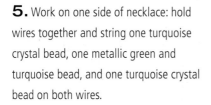

Forget-Me-Not Bracelet

This project features a unique design in which the clasp is made with two strands of beads.

Materials and Tools

- five 10mm handmade forget-me-not flower beads (page 32), amber and blue, round
- one 10mm dark amber crystal bead, faceted round
- six 6mm aquamarine crystal beads, faceted round
- thirty-four 3mm gold seed beads
- six 5mm sky blue glass beads, round
- one gold head pin
- three gold crimp beads

- one 16" (41 cm) silicon beading thread
- wire-cutters
- round-nose pliers
- flat-nose pliers

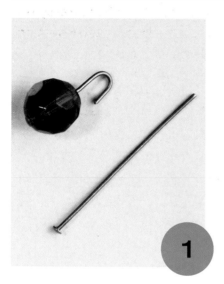

2. String decorated head pin onto beading thread and draw to middle of thread.

3. String one aquamarine crystal bead and one gold seed bead on one side of thread. String two gold seed beads and one sky blue glass bead on other side of thread.

1. String dark amber crystal bead onto head pin. Trim head pin and form a loop.

4. Hold ends of thread together and string one handmade flower bead onto both threads. Hold threads apart and string one gold seed bead and one aquamarine crystal bead on one thread; string one sky blue glass bead and two gold seed beads on other thread.

5. Repeat step 4 another four times.

6. Hold threads together and string one crimp bead. Draw crimp bead along until it is flush with other beads and flatten.

7. Hold threads apart and string four gold seed beads on each thread. Hold threads together and string one crimp bead. Draw crimp bead along until it is flush with other beads and flatten.

8. Hold threads apart and string four gold seed beads on each thread.

9. Hold threads together and string one crimp bead. Draw crimp bead along until it is flush with other beads. Flatten crimp bead and trim thread.

Lavender and Rose Cube Bracelet

When selecting the chain for this bracelet, make
sure it is thin enough to fit through the holes in the
gold and handmade beads.

Materials and Tools

- three 15mm handmade misted cube beads (page 44), various shades of pink
- three 15mm handmade tri-color cube beads (page 42), various shades of pink
- twelve 3mm fuchsia seed beads
- six 6mm pink crystal beads, faceted round
- six 6mm antique gold beads, round
- one antique gold elephant charm
- one antique gold heart charm
- six antique gold head pins
- two-piece antique gold clasp
- ten antique gold jump rings
- one 8½" (22 cm) small-link antique gold chain
- wire cutters
- round-nose pliers

1. String one fuchsia seed bead, one pink crystal bead, and one fuchsia seed bead on a head pin. Trim head pin and form a loop.

2. Repeat step 1 another five times.

3. Open a jump ring and string on elephant charm. String jump ring through last chain link in chain and close jump ring.

4. Count eight links from this end of chain. Open a jump ring and string onto link. String on a decorated head pin and close jump ring.

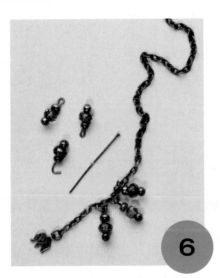

6

5. Count two links along chain. Open a jump ring and string onto link. String on a decorated head pin and close jump ring.

6. Repeat step 5 another two times.

7. Decide order of handmade beads before stringing bracelet. String one antique gold bead and one handmade misted cube bead onto chain.

8. String one antique gold bead and one handmade tri-color cube bead onto chain.

(continued)

9. Repeat steps 7 and 8 another two times.

10. Open a jump ring and draw it through a link that is halfway between elephant charm (at beginning of bracelet) and first decorated head pin. String half of clasp onto jump ring and close jump ring

11. Measure bracelet around wrist. Open a jump ring, string on other half of clasp, and string through appropriate link in bracelet. Close jump ring.

12. Open three jump rings and string each jump ring through loop in a decorated head pin. Affix decorated head pins to chain, between clasp and end of chain.

13. Open a jump ring and string through heart charm. String jump ring through last link at end of bracelet and close jump ring.

Porcupine Bracelet

Make this bracelet as colorful as you like by creating handmade beads in a variety of colors. You can make dots with identical or complementary colors.

Materials and Tools

- one 13mm handmade encased gold leaf bead (page 34), cylindrical
- nine 10 x 15mm handmade porcupine beads (page 21), various colors
- eleven 6mm transparent yellow with gold core crystal beads, faceted round
- six 7mm antique gold flower beads, round
- ten 6mm orange crystal beads, faceted round
- ten 3mm antique gold seed beads
- one gold head pin
- two gold crimp beads
- one 16" (41 cm) silicon beading thread
- wire-cutters
- round-nose pliers
- flat-nose pliers

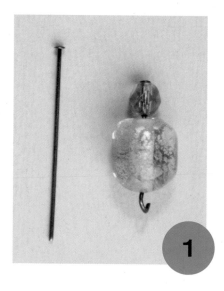

1

1. String one transparent yellow with gold core crystal bead and handmade encased gold leaf bead onto head pin. Trim head pin and form a loop.

2. String decorated head pin onto beading thread and draw along to middle of thread.

3. Hold ends of thread together and string one crimp bead. Draw crimp bead along until it is flush with head pin and flatten.

4. Decide order of handmade porcupine beads before stringing bracelet. Hold ends of thread together and string one antique gold flower bead and one handmade porcupine bead.

5

5. Hold threads apart and string one transparent yellow with gold core crystal bead and one orange crystal bead on one thread; string one orange crystal bead and one transparent yellow with gold core crystal bead on other thread.

6. Hold threads together and string one handmade porcupine bead, one antique gold flower bead, and one handmade porcupine bead on both threads.

7. Repeat steps 5 and 6 four times.

8. Hold threads together and string one antique gold flower bead and one crimp bead on both threads. Draw crimp bead along until it is flush with other beads, and flatten.

9. Hold threads apart and string five gold beads on each thread. Hold threads together and string one crimp bead onto both threads. Draw crimp bead along until it is flush with other beads. Flatten crimp bead and trim thread.

Meadows of Green and White Necklace

This bright necklace, with handmade beads decorated in a freehand style, is an excellent expression of your own style.

Materials and Tools

- seven handmade freehand decorated beads (page 29), in the following colors and sizes:
    - one 20 x 9mm green and ivory, bicone
    - two 20 x 9mm green with ivory, cylindrical
    - four 20 x 9mm ivory with green, cylindrical
- twenty-eight 6mm dark emerald crystal beads, faceted round
- six 10mm light emerald crystal beads, faceted round

- four 5mm antique gold double-disk beads
- ten 5mm antique gold disk beads,

- four 4mm antique gold round beads
- eight 3mm antique gold seed beads
- two gold crimp beads
- two antique gold jump rings
- one antique gold clasp
- two 22" (56 cm) 18-gauge gold-filled half-hard wires
- flat-nose pliers
- wire cutters

---

1. Hold wires together and string handmade freehand decorated bead (bicone) onto both wires. Draw bead to middle of wires.

2

2. Work on one side of necklace: hold wires together and string one dark emerald crystal, one light emerald crystal, one handmade freehand decorated bead (cylindrical, green with ivory), one antique gold double-disk bead, one handmade freehand decorated bead (cylindrical, ivory with green), one dark emerald crystal, one light emerald crystal, and one handmade freehand decorated bead (cylindrical, ivory with green) on both wires.

3. String one antique gold double-disk bead and one light emerald crystal bead.

4. String one dark emerald crystal bead, one antique gold disk bead, one dark emerald crystal bead, one antique gold disk bead, one dark emerald crystal, one antique gold disk bead, and one antique gold round bead.

(continued)

5. Repeat step 4.

6. String one antique gold seed bead and one dark emerald crystal.

7. Repeat step 6 another two times.

8. String one antique gold seed bead and one crimp bead. Draw crimp bead along until it is flush with other beads. Make a loop in wires and draw ends back through crimp bead. Flatten crimp bead and trim wires.

9. Open a jump ring and string into loop. String half of clasp onto jump ring and close jump ring.

10. Repeat steps 2 to 9 on other side of necklace. Open other jump ring and string through loop. String other half of clasp onto jump ring and close jump ring.

Turquoise and Coral Harvest Necklace

Using real turquoise and coral beads in this necklace brings out the color of the glass in these handmade beads.

Materials and Tools

- nine 15mm handmade eye beads (page 30), ivory with orange and blue, round
- twenty-eight 12 x 4mm turquoise chip beads
- twenty-eight 10 x 4mm coral beads, eye-shaped
- eighteen 3mm ivory seed beads
- two gold crimp beads
- two gold jump rings
- one gold clasp

- two 20" (51 cm) 18-gauge gold-filled half-hard wires
- flat-nose pliers
- wire cutters

1. Hold wires together and string one handmade eye bead onto both wires. Draw bead to middle of wires.

2. Work on one side of necklace: hold wires apart and string one turquoise chip bead onto one wire; string one coral bead onto other wire. Hold wires together and string one handmade eye bead onto both wires.

3. Repeat step 2 another three times.

4. Repeat steps 2 and 3 on other side of necklace.

5. Work on one side of necklace: hold wires apart and string one turquoise chip bead onto one wire, string one coral bead onto other wire. Hold wires together and string one ivory seed bead onto both wires.

7. Open a jump ring and string into loop. String half of clasp through jump ring and close jump ring.

8. Repeat steps 5 and 6 on other side of necklace. Open a jump ring and string through loop. String other half of clasp through jump ring and close jump ring.

6. Repeat step 5 another five times. Hold wires together and string three ivory seed beads onto both wires. String one crimp bead and draw it along until it is flush with other beads. Make a loop in wires and draw ends back through crimp bead. Flatten crimp bead and trim wires bead.

Swirls of Twirls Necklace

This necklace is simple and sweet, and the beads look good enough to eat!

Materials and Tools

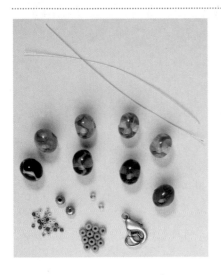

- sixteen 12mm handmade swirled stripe beads (page 54), various colors, round
- forty-five 3mm turquoise seed beads
- thirty 1mm yellow seed beads
- thirty 1mm green seed beads
- thirty 1mm orange seed beads
- two 6mm dotted silver beads, round
- two silver crimp beads
- two silver jump rings
- one silver clasp

- two 22" (56 cm) 18-gauge silver-filled half-hard wires
- wire-cutters
- flat-nose pliers

1. Decide order of handmade swirled stripe beads before stringing necklace. You'll need four groups of three handmade beads for middle of necklace, and one pair of handmade beads at each end. Hold wires together and string middle handmade swirled stripe bead onto both wires. Draw bead to middle of wires.

2. Work on one side of necklace: hold wires together and string one turquoise seed bead and one handmade swirled stripe bead.

3. Repeat step 2 on other side of necklace.

4. Work on one side of necklace: hold wires apart and string one turquoise seed bead, one yellow seed bead, one green seed bead, and one turquoise seed bead on each wire.

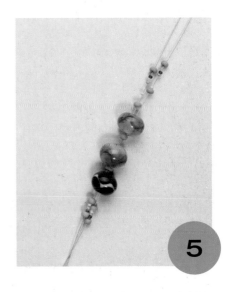

5

5. Repeat step 4 on other side of necklace.

6. Work on one side of necklace: hold wires together and string one swirled stripe bead, one turquoise seed bead, one swirled stripe bead, one turquoise seed bead, and one swirled stripe bead.

(continued)

9. Repeat steps 6 and 7 on other side of necklace.

10. Work on one side of necklace: hold wires together and string one turquoise seed bead; hold wires apart and string one yellow seed bead, one orange seed bead, and one green seed bead on each wire separately. Repeat step 9 another three times.

11. Hold wires together and string four turquoise seed beads. Hold wires apart and string one yellow seed bead, one orange seed bead, and one green seed bead on each wire separately. Hold wires together and string four turquoise seed beads, and one dotted silver bead.

12. String one crimp bead and draw it along wires until it is flush with other beads. Make a loop in wires and draw ends back through crimp bead. Flatten crimp bead and trim wires.

7. Hold wires apart and string one turquoise seed bead, one yellow seed bead, one orange seed bead, one green seed bead, and one turquoise seed bead onto each wire.

8. Hold wires together and string one swirled stripe bead. Hold wires apart and string one turquoise seed bead, one green seed bead, one orange seed bead, one yellow seed bead, and one turquoise seed bead onto each wire. Hold wires together and string one swirled stripe bead.

13. Open a jump ring and string through loop. String half of clasp through jump ring and close jump ring.

14. Repeat steps 9 to 13 on other side of necklace. Open other jump ring and string through loop. String other half of clasp onto jump ring and close jump ring.

Fairy Leaf Necklace

With its transparent, leaf-shaped beads, there's a touch of fairy magic in this delicate necklace.

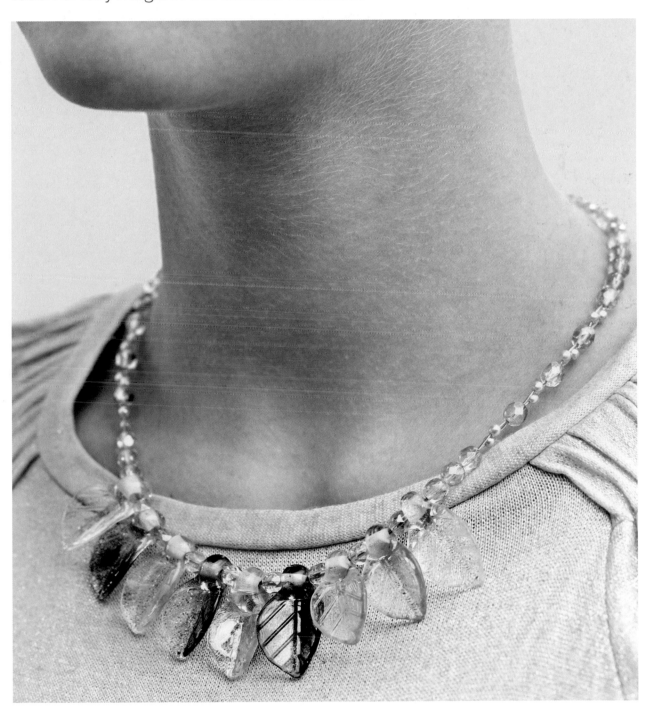

Materials and Tools

- nine handmade textured leaf beads (page 52), in the following colors and sizes:
  - one 10mm transparent with gold leaf
  - eight 10mm transparent green, purple, and blue
- thirty-four 6mm transparent light amber crystal beads, faceted round
- thirty-six 3mm pearl beads
- six 6mm transparent with gold-core crystal beads, faceted round

- two 6mm light pink crystal beads, faceted round
- two gold crimp beads
- two gold jump rings
- one gold clasp
- three 18" (46 cm) 18-gauge gold-filled half-hard wires
- flat-nose pliers
- wire cutters

1. Decide order of handmade textured leaf beads before stringing necklace. Hold wires together and string handmade textured leaf with gold leaf bead on all three wires. Draw bead to middle of wires. String one transparent light amber crystal bead on each side of gold leaf bead.

2. Work on one side of necklace: hold wires together and string one handmade textured leaf bead.

3. String one transparent light amber crystal bead and one handmade textured leaf bead.

4. Repeat step 3 another two times.

5. Work on other side of necklace: string one handmade colored leaf bead, then repeat step 3 another three times.

8. Hold wires together and string one transparent light amber crystal bead, three transparent with gold core crystal beads, and one transparent light amber crystal bead. Hold wires apart and string one pearl bead on each wire. Hold wires together and string one transparent light amber crystal beads. Hold wires apart and string one pearl bead on each wire. Hold wires together and string five transparent light amber crystal beads.

9. Hold wires together and string one crimp bead onto all three wires. Make a loop in wires and draw ends back through crimp bead. Flatten crimp bead and trim wires.

10. Open a jump ring and string into loop. String clasp onto jump ring and close jump ring.

11. Repeat steps 5 to 9 on other side of necklace. Open a jump ring, string onto loop, and close jump ring.

6. Work on one side of necklace: hold all three wires together, and string three transparent light amber crystal beads. Hold wires apart and string one pearl bead on each wire. Hold wires together and string one light pink crystal bead Hold wires apart and string one pearl bead on each wire.

7. Hold wires together and string one transparent light amber crystal bead. Hold wires apart and string one pearl bead on each wire. Hold wires together and string one transparent light amber crystal. Hold wires apart and string one pearl bead on each wire.

Lemony Lime Enamel Necklace

This design is bright and refreshing. If you choose a different color of enamel for your handmade beads, select complementary seed beads.

Materials and Tools

- nine 15mm handmade powdered enamel beads (see page 58), ivory with mustard and burgundy, round
- six 7mm handmade flush dotted beads (see page 21), yellow with green
- twelve 3mm petroleum green seed beads
- eighteen 3mm yellow with green core seed beads
- fifteen silver eye pins
- four silver jump rings
- one silver clasp
- one 4" (10 cm) silver link chain, consisting of links that can be opened
- round-nose pliers
- wire cutters

1. String one petroleum green seed bead, one handmade flush dotted bead, and one petroleum green seed bead on an eye pin. Trim eye pin and form a loop.

2. Repeat step 1 another five times.

3. String one yellow with green core seed bead, one handmade enamel bead, and one yellow with green core seed bead on an eye pin. Trim eye pin and form a loop.

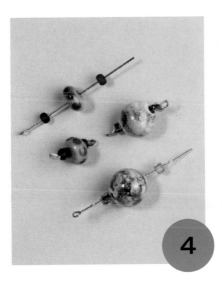

4

4. Repeat step 3 another eight times.

5. Open second link from one end of chain and remove two links from chain.

6. String open link into one loop of a decorated eye pin and close link.

7. Repeat step 5, then string open link into loop at other end of same decorated eye pin. Close link.

8. Repeat steps 5 to 7 another fourteen times.

(continued)

9. Decide order of decorated eye pins in an alternating pattern of enamel beads and flush dotted beads. Arrange two eye pins with enamel beads at both ends of necklace.

10. Open outer links on right side of all decorated eye pins and string through outer link on left side of adjacent eye pins to attach all decorated eye pins.

11. Fold remaining chain in half and open middle link, making two even chains.

12. Open a jump ring and string through last link at one end of necklace. Attach one piece of chain and close jump ring.

13. Open another jump ring and string through last link of chain. Attach clasp to jump ring and close jump ring.

14. Open a jump ring and string through last link at other end of necklace. Attach other piece of chain and close jump ring. Open a jump ring, string through last link of chain, and close jump ring.

Lucky Eye Charm Bracelet

You'll have good luck wherever you go with a wrist full of these bright beads, reminiscent of talismans used to ward of the evil eye.

Materials and Tools

- seven 15mm handmade beautiful blue eyes beads (page 48), dark blue, light blue, and purple, round
- four handmade round beads (page 16), in the following colors and sizes:
    - two 10mm transparent light blue
    - two 10mm light lapis
- fifty 3mm silver seed beads
- three 8mm shiny cobalt blue beads, round
- five 6mm cobalt blue crystal beads, faceted round
- two 10mm cobalt blue crystal beads, faceted round

- thirteen 10mm silver charms, various shapes
- eleven silver eye pins
- ten silver head pins
- thirty-four silver jump rings
- one silver clasp
- one 8½" (22 cm) large link silver chain
- wire cutters
- round-nose pliers

---

1. String one silver seed bead, one handmade blue-eyed bead, and one silver seed bead onto an eye pin. Trim eye pin and form a loop.

2. Repeat step 1 another six times.

3. String one silver seed bead, one handmade round bead, and one silver seed bead onto an eye pin. Trim eye pin and form a loop.

4. Repeat step 3 another three times.

5. String one shiny cobalt blue bead and two silver seed beads onto a head pin. Trim head pin and form a loop.

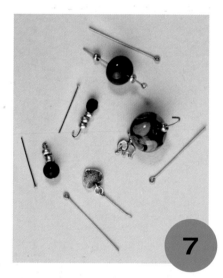

7

6. Repeat step 5, using various combinations of seed beads, cobalt blue beads, and crystals, another nine times.

7. Open a jump ring and string onto bottom loop of a decorated eye pin. String one charm onto jump ring and close jump ring.

8. Repeat step 7 another ten times.

9. Open a jump ring and string onto top loop of a decorated eye pin.

10. Repeat step 9 another ten times.

11. Open a jump ring and string through loop in a decorated head pin.

12. Repeat step 11 another nine times.

13. Decide order of decorated head pins and eye pins. String jump ring from middle pin to middle of chain and then close jump ring.

14. Leave even spaces on either side of middle decorated pin, and affix next decorated pins on either side.

15. Repeat step 14 until all decorated pins are attached to chain.

16. Open a jump ring and string through a charm. String jump ring through last link at one end of bracelet and close jump ring.

17. Open other jump ring and string through clasp. String through last link at other end of bracelet and close jump ring. String a jump ring through remaining charm, string through link near this end of bracelet, and close jump ring.

Resources

United States

1 Stop Bead Shop
JoAnn's Shopping Center
2752 Festival Lane
Columbus, OH 43017
Website: www.1stopbeadshop.com
Email: info@1stopbeadshop.com
Phone: 614.573.6452
Lampwork beads, tools, and classes

Alley Cat Beads
11928 N. Washington Street
Northglenn, CO 80233
Website: www.alleycatbeads.com
Email: info@alleycatbeads.com
Phone: 303.451.1900
Beads, tools, and classes

Arrow Springs
4301 Product Drive
Shingle Springs, CA 95682
Website: www.arrowsprings.com
Email: flameon@ArrowSprings.com
Phone: 800.899.0689
Tools, beads, classes, and kits

Auntie's Beads
406 South Main Street
Grapevine, TX 76051
Website: www.auntiesbeads.com
Email: auntiesbeads@yahoo.com
Phone: 866.26BEADS (866.262.3237)
Supplies, glass, and lampwork beads

Barbara Becker Simon
122 SW 46th Terrace
Cape Coral, FL 33914
Website: www.bbsimon.com
Email: barbara@bbsimon.com
Phone: 239.549.5971
Beadmaking classes

Frantz Art Glass and Supply
130 W. Corporate Road
Shelton, WA 98584
Website: www.frantzartglass.com
Email: supplies@frantzartglass.com
Phone: 800.839.6712
Tools, books, and videos

Sundance Art Glass
6052 Foster Road
Paradise, CA 95969
Website: www.sundanceglass.com
Phone: 888.446.8452
Supplies, classes, and workshops

Venetian Bead Shop
1008 Stuart Drive
Santa Clara, CA 95051
Website: www.venetianbeadshop.com
Phone: 800.439.3551
Lampwork beads, tools, and supplies

International

beadFX Inc
128 Manville Road Suite #9
Scarborough, ON M1L 4J5
Canada
Website: www.beadfx.com
Email: info@beadfx.com
Phone: 416.701.1373
Lampwork beads, tools, and classes

Benjamin's Crafts
868 Beaufort Street
Inglewood WA 6052
Australia
Phone: (08) 9370 2132
Beads and beading supplies

Jewel Toolcraft
35 Spencer Street
Hockley
Birmingham, United Kingdom
B18 6DE
Website: www.jewel-toolcraft.co.uk
Email: jewlsandtools@tiscali.co.uk
Phone: +0121 212 2446
Glass beads and tools

Koralky Beads
Vinohradská street Nr. 76, Prague 2
Prague, Czech Republic
Website: www.koralky.net
Email: info@koralky.net
Phone: 604845737
Beads and beading supplies

Metissage Toulouse
11 rue cujas 31000
Toulouse, France
Website: www.onlinebeads.net
Phone: +0562308009
Beads and beading supplies